Learning
From
Other
Women

Learning From Other Women

How to Benefit From the Knowledge, Wisdom, and Experience of Female Mentors

Carolyn Duff

AMACOM

American Management Association

New York • Atlanta • Boston • Chicago • Kansas City • San Francisco • Washington, D.C.
Brussels • Mexico City • Tokyo • Toronto

Special discounts on bulk quantities of AMACOM books are available to corporations, professional associations, and other organizations. For details, contact Special Sales Department, AMACOM, an imprint of AMA Publications, a division of
American Management Association,
1601 Broadway, New York, NY 10019.
Tel.: 212-903-8316   Fax: 212-903-8083

This publication is designed to provide accurate and authoritative information in regard to the subject matter covered. It is sold with the understanding that the publisher is not engaged in rendering legal, accounting, or other professional service. If legal advice or other expert assistance is required, the services of a competent professional person should be sought.

Library of Congress Cataloging-in-Publication Data

Duff, Carolyn S., 1941–
    Learning from other women : how to benefit from the knowledge, wisdom, and experience of female mentors / Carolyn Duff.
        p.   cm.
    Includes bibliographical references and index.
    ISBN 0-8144-0455-3
    1. Women in the professions—United States.   2. Mentoring in the professions—United States.   3. Businesswomen—United States.
4. Mentoring in business—United States.   I. Title.
HD6054.2.U6D84   1999
658.4'09'082—dc21   99-28081
                                                                                    CIP

Printing number

10   9   8   7   6   5   4   3   2   1

To
Lauralyn, Nancy, and **Jen,**
wonderful young women who are
building our tomorrow.

Contents

Acknowledgments   *xi*

Introduction   *xiii*

Chapter 1
The Value of Women as Mentors for
Women   1
DEBBIE'S STORY   1
Why You Need Women Mentors   4
    A Place to Be Whole   4
    A Place to Be Authentic   5
    Women Know the Waters   6
    Women Can Help You Move Ahead   8
Women Are in Place to Become Your Mentors   9
Women Are Willing to Be Your Learning Partners   9
How You Can Use This Book to Learn From Women   11
If You Want to Learn More   12

Chapter 2
Confronting the Myths and Fears That
Have Kept Women Apart   13
Fear of Appearing Demanding, Needy, and Weak   13
MEGAN'S STORY   13
The Myth That You Will Be Rejected   16
The Myth That Women "Owe You Something"   18
The Myth of the "Dead Even" Rule   19
The Myth of the Queen Bee   21
The Myth of the Destructive Woman and Other
    Women-Can't-Work-With-Women Stereotypes   23

Contents

Taking Your Pulse on Woman-to-Woman
    Relationships   26
If You Want to Learn More   29

Chapter 3
A Woman's Way of Mentoring: Entering the Gift Exchange   31
JAN AND BETTY   31
Progressing From the Male Mentoring Tradition   32
New Dimensions for Woman-to-Woman Mentoring   34
The Essence of Woman-to-Woman Mentoring
    Connections   37
Relationship: The Foundation of Woman-to-
    Woman Mentoring   37
Goals for Mentoring in the Female Form   38
Mutual Learning as a Gift Exchange   40
If You Want to Learn More   44

Chapter 4
Recognizing the Gift: Five Forms of the Woman-to-Woman Mentoring Connection   45
KAIA AND DARCY   45
Finding the Most Comfortable Fit   47
When You Say Mentor and She Says Friend   47
In All but Name: The Unnamed Coach, Counselor,
    Advocate   50
The Informal Named Mentoring Connection   53
Assigned Mentors in Formal Mentoring Programs   55
Cross-Organizational Formal Mentoring
    Opportunities   58
The Right Connection for You   59
If You Want to Learn More   60

Chapter 5
Preparing to Be a Protégé   61
LANIE'S STORY   61
Not One, but Many!   63
Becoming a Responsible Protégé   65
How to Prepare   65
Are You Ready?   66

Learning From an Accomplished Woman 68
Appreciating Hierarchy 69
Getting Ready for the Critique 70
Can You Do Your Part? 71
Supporting Her in Public 73
When She Is Simply Too Busy 73
What About Your Boss and Your Coworkers? 74
What Mentors Want You to Know 76
   Have Specific Goals 77
   Help Your Mentor Focus Constructive Feedback 79
   Support Your Mentor with Positive Comments to
     Your Colleagues and to Her Bosses 80
   Put the Mentoring Into Action! 80
   Respond to Opportunities! 81
   Don't Expect a Promotion 81
Say Thank You When You Say Good Bye 82
If You Want to Learn More 82

Chapter 6
Identifying the Woman to Be Your Mentor 83
   MARCIE'S STORY 83
Who Should Be Your Mentor? 85
Is She a Woman I Admire? 87
   KINSEY'S AND JACKIE'S STORY 88
Is She in the Loop? 89
Values are Important 90
Asking a Woman to Mentor You 96
The First Approach 96
Evaluating Your Mentor 98
How to Leave Your Mentor 102
If You Want to Learn More 104

Chapter 7
Protecting Your Protégé/Mentor
Relationship 105
   LAURALYN'S STORY 105
Protecting the Mentoring Experience 107
Managing the Friendship Issue 107

Remembering That Your Mentor Isn't Your Mother 111
Respecting Different Choices 113
Anticipating Competition 116
Honoring the Gift 119
If You Want to Learn More 120

Chapter 8
Expanding the Possibilities: Additional
Opportunities for Learning From Women 121
    Susan's Story 121
    Short-Term Mentors 122
    Peer Mentors 123
    Horizontal Mentoring 127
    Mentoring Groups 128
    Weekend Mentoring 131
    Coaches for Hire 132
    If You Want to Learn More 136

Chapter 9
Extending the Wisdom 139
    Networks 140
    Corporate Networks and Forums 140
    Going Beyond the Corporate Boundaries 144
    Ethnic Groups and Networks 146
    Action Groups and Power Groups 149
    Affinity Groups That Enhance Our Experience as
        Women 151
    Our Future Learning Together 154
    If You Want to Learn More 157

Bibliography 159

Index 165

Acknowledgments

MUCH OF THIS book comes from the knowledge and experience of more than two hundred women who gave me their time, their stories, their insights, and their encouragement. I would like to list every name and the names of the businesses, corporations, and professional settings that supported my research, but I respect their concern for confidentiality. However, you will recognize your story, and thank you.

Thank you, also, to Michael Cohn for his support and his determination. And my family: To my husband, Bill, an engineering professor, who read and thoughtfully edited material quite outside his normal arena; Ethan, who understands frustration, persistence, and celebration; Duffer for a respectful balance of interest and distance; Lauralyn for her prodding and for her sharing; and to my mother, Ruth Searing, who died before this project was complete—I thank her for her belief.

Introduction

THIS BOOK EXISTS to encourage you to reach out, to reach up, and to benefit from the deep resources of experience and wisdom that women have to offer for your career and your life. These women should be your mentors: the teachers, guides, coaches, and counselors who can enhance your development and advance your career opportunities.

At work, women have been mentored by men, in the male tradition, producing results that reflect and perpetuate the existing system. Certainly not all, but many women have been encouraged to assimilate, to adapt to a way of being and a reward structure that perpetuate male expectations and values. Adapting in this way allowed a generation of women to survive and succeed in a career or profession. But for many women the male-structured workplace did not feel like home, a place where they could be their genuine, whole selves.

Today these women have their experiences and their wisdom to share. They have struggled to balance their desire for career success with their need to be themselves and to create a life that challenges all their potentials, as highly competent professionals and as full and complete women.

I talked to more than two hundred women while gathering information for this book. Women who have been mentors and protégés told me about their experiences learning from men and with women. Protégés at an early stage in their careers shared with me their hesitations and their hopes for woman-to-woman mentoring connections. I visited with mentoring pairs who were open about the frustrations and profound gifts in their relationships. I attended women's forums, networks, affinity groups, and action workshops. I watched and participated as women reached out to teach and learn together. And I am excited by the energy, goodwill, and powerful possibilities of these learning opportunities.

Susan Skogg, author of *Embracing Our Essence: Spiritual Conversations With Prominent Women,* is a truly generous and informed woman who mentors by sharing her knowledge and insight through her books, her talks, and conversations. Over lunch with me at Pelican Fish, I asked her why, when the introduction to her book cited mostly male spiritual guides, she decided to "tap the wisdom of more experienced female seekers" and not include men among her storytellers. Susan answered that her decision was "instinctive." She assumed "that women could teach me what I needed to learn better than a man could." A woman, Susan believed, would be closer to her in experience and spirit. Women's spiritual stories and wisdom, the voice of the feminine, are still overlooked in our culture, she believes. "When women want to discover their true nature," she continued, "they must go to women and form a supportive kinship." Women, Susan has learned, come together for affirmation. "In all my readings," Susan says, "it is the women's voices that ring truest for me."

You need to be mentored by women who will recognize and understand you as you will identify with and understand them. You need the woman connection to grow as your authentic self in a workplace that you and your women guides will redefine and redesign to reflect your values and support your fulfillment.

But a book just about women as mentors for women? What about men? Can't men be good mentors too?

Many women have challenged me with these questions. Yes, men can be wonderful career mentors for you, and men and women do mentor successfully together. You can have, and you should have, men who can provide information, coaching, opportunity, and support for your professional development.

However, men have not shared the female experience. Most men cannot guide you in the wholeness of your female self as you make your career decisions and respond to your workplace and life challenges. It is difficult for many women to expose the full range of their female selves in a woman/man mentoring relationship. We hold back some of who we are to achieve a middle ground where both of us are comfortable. We deny ourselves our wholeness.

Haven't women always turned to other women for wisdom and guidance in how we approach and live our lives?

Yes, women have passed on their experience and their understanding to new generations of women. However, this learning has often taken place without being named. It has happened when friends talk with friends about their job and career plans, and when mothers and aunts gather in the kitchen and discuss the implications of births, deaths, and other changes in the patterns of life. It has happened when women at work come together for coffee, meet in the hall, travel together for meetings in another city.

We have not, however, always asked experienced and knowledgeable women: Can you help me? Can I learn with you? Some of us are waiting to reach out, but we have not wanted to be too presumptuous and intrude in another woman's career and life. You may, for your part, have demurred from asking a woman to mentor you because of the obligations involved and because you did not wish to demand time, attention, and effort.

I encourage you to ask for the mentoring you want and need. And you must be prepared to enter a gift exchange when you are mentored. Woman-to-woman mentoring is mutual and reciprocal. You will receive gifts of experience and wisdom, and you will give gifts of your perceptions and your support.

But if women have always learned from women, why do we need to learn about being protégés of women at work?

Women mentoring women in the workplace is a relatively new phenomenon. Woman-to-woman mentoring encompasses circumstances and rules that are specific to a female style and representative of a female culture. The workplace puts demands on our priorities and our energy that bring new factors into woman-to-woman relationships. Our identity as professional women with career responsibilities affects our interactions with other women who are also committed to improving their performance and achieving greater success. Women learning from women at work, women mentoring each other as career professionals with job and personal lives, is an emerging opportunity with enormous potential to change work and women's lives for the future. You need to be prepared to approach your mentoring relationships for the best advantage. You need to understand the potentials and respect the new rules for successful, rewarding woman-to-woman mentoring connections.

Your woman mentors are your guides for the future. You will learn together to build careers and lives based on what you value and how you want to succeed.

Learning
From
Other
Women

CHAPTER 1

The Value of Women as Mentors for Women

Today, as a woman aspiring to a fulfilled life of career and personal achievement, you have available to you a rich and well-positioned resource: other women. These experienced women are waiting and willing to support you as teachers, coaches, counselors, guides, and advocates. They will share their wisdom and introduce you to people and opportunities. They, and you, will discover that through woman-to-woman learning relationships, all women benefit, both individually and as contributors to a strong network of women vested in the future.

What you will learn from women will enhance your career. Women as mentors and learning partners will also guide and support you in achieving your whole-life goals. What you experience in your woman-to-woman learning relationships will affirm your power as a woman—to be and to achieve as an authentic, complete female person.

DEBBIE'S STORY

Debbie is a bright, friendly young woman with a spontaneous laugh and the discipline to focus intently on the situation at hand. At age 33 she is a regional customer group leader for a large national company. Debbie has sought and appreciated the support of influential male mentors as she has moved around the country and ahead in her career. "In fact," she told me, "I consciously avoided women who might have been mentors. I didn't

1

think they could give me what I needed to learn. I thought they wouldn't be able to connect me with the inside track."

During her regional moves, Debbie had been aware of a woman, Anna, who was ten years older and always a few management levels ahead of her. When they traveled to the same meetings, they would talk, and the talk often involved changes at work, company direction, and opportunities for advancement. Debbie liked what she saw of Anna's management style and admired the reputation for good performance that Anna had developed within the company. Anna often punctuated their conversations with funny, affectionate stories about her two young children. She seemed comfortable leaving them when she traveled, although she acknowledged missing the bedtime routines that her husband oversaw in her absence.

After five years of postponing the decision, Debbie and her husband, an employee of the same company, decided to have a child, and Debbie became pregnant. She had not told anyone at work, and she was reluctant to discuss her situation with her male mentors for fear she "wouldn't present it right, or they wouldn't understand what I wanted and needed to know." Debbie acknowledges that she was feeling frustrated and didn't know where to get the information and guidance she needed. Then, at a luncheon meeting, Debbie saw Anna and took a seat next to the senior woman. Anna was immediately friendly and welcoming, asking Debbie about her work and Debbie's growing span of responsibility. Anna seemed so comfortable with her career and content with her family that Debbie found herself telling Anna that she was pregnant and asking if she could arrange a meeting with Anna to explore her choices concerning how to manage both her new family and the career she valued. Anna agreed, and they continued their lunch conversation with stories about Anna's first pregnancy and how her boss had reacted and how she managed, after three months of maternity leave, the stress, challenge, loneliness, and exhilaration of reentry.

Debbie met with Anna the next week and came away elated and encouraged. The context for their exchange was work, specifically in the insurance company culture, and Debbie's decision to combine a family with her career. The conversation had a business intent and a career focus, but Debbie didn't feel that she had to consciously separate her work self from the other dimensions of her life in presenting her concerns to Anna. "I felt that I was really being myself with Anna," Debbie told me during one of our phone conversations. "I wasn't on guard, being careful to appear totally work-focused. Our conversation that day and in the sessions that have followed was open and honest. Anna listens and is inquisitive in a way that prompts me to see connections and options I might have missed on my own.

"I am comfortable going to Anna without the perfectly formed questions I prepare for my male mentors," Debbie continued. "I can be comfortable not being sure of myself, wondering aloud about how certain circumstances might change my decisions. Anna seems to take in the whole picture and helps me see how my choices will affect my future with the company. She doesn't put pressure on me to do what she did. She is concerned that I make the right decisions for myself."

In fact, Anna has become a supporter and advocate for Debbie as well as a guide. She recognizes Debbie's abilities and dedication and wants to see Debbie advance to greater responsibility and influence. As vice president and regional branch manager, Anna is in a position to create assignments and schedules for Debbie that, after she returns from maternity leave, will bring her immediate visibility and allow her to take appropriate advantage of the company's family-friendly policies. Debbie told me enthusiastically, "The experience with Anna has been so positive, so friendly yet professional, that I have asked if I can consider her my mentor and continue our conversations. She agrees and says she is learning as much as I am from our relationship."

Debbie is a woman who has discovered the advantage of having a woman mentor as a valuable part of her career network. At first reluctant to identify and be identified with a woman, Debbie now realizes that through her learning connection with Anna, she has tapped a resource that will help her achieve satisfaction by reaching her performance goals at work and her personal goals for a complete and fulfilling life. In her conversations with Anna, she will be known and appreciated as a whole person with a life that includes her career, her family, and her individual passions and pursuits. The mentoring she will receive from Anna will acknowledge the value of an integrated self while directing her to achieve and advance within a career she loves.

What Debbie will gain as a person in her career and her life will be greatly enhanced by the acceptance of her female self she is experiencing with Anna. As a mentor, Anna can help Debbie achieve at work. As a woman mentor, she can also help Debbie live well with what she achieves.

Why You Need Women Mentors

Women need women as mentors because only women can truly empathize with the experience of being a woman. We need women mentors because with other women we can act and feel and give as our true selves. In return, we will grow in confidence, strength, and accomplishment. Women will guide us toward the wholeness that is our vision and our future.

A Place to Be Whole

You need women mentors to help you discover and develop your full potential as both a professional and a woman. With them you can be an attorney, a CPA, a marketing director, or a project manager at the same time you are a mother, a romantic partner, a community activist, a daughter, and a sister.

You will not have to explain to a woman what it means to be female with a career within a life.

With a woman you can open a dialogue that includes all aspects of your lives. She will empathize with the difficulty and the goal because she will have faced similar choices. She will share with you what she has learned and what she is still learning.

When you find women as mentors, you will be inviting them into a gift exchange. You will learn from them, and together you will hone the abilities and the focus that can provide work satisfaction, good performance, and life rewards. Through the gift exchange, the women who mentor you will become vested in your achievement and your success. You will then extend these gifts to others, and together you will build a women's network based on mutual learning, caring, encouragement, opportunity, and support.

Debbie found Anna as her mentor. You, too, will find the right women at the right time. When you do, they will enhance your career and enrich your life.

A Place to Be Authentic

You can feel comfortable giving open expression to your full range of thinking, being, and reacting with your women mentors. In a woman-to-woman mentoring exchange, you can be comfortable about expressing and sharing your feelings. Feelings can be highly emotionally charged and resistant to rational, linear logic. For me, and for many women, the emotional intensity associated with experience makes that experience real. I was fortunate fifteen years ago to have a sensitive woman mentor who understood my emotional attachment to teaching and my fears about leaving the classroom and entering into a business partnership. She let me be sad and scared and excited and hopeful—all the while helping me find within myself the grounding I needed for the new venture. By contrast, with my male advisers, I was conscious of focusing my questions on business issues and keeping my emotional concerns at bay. Dr. Exavier Amadoir, director of the Diagnosis and Evaluation Center at Columbia University and New York State Psychological Institute, has reported that when women open up and share their feelings with someone else, they feel comfortable and good, and their esteem goes up. By contrast, expression of feelings, especially with work associates, often makes many men feel awkward and uncomfortable. When we respect this propensity on the part of our male colleagues and mentors, we hold back part of who we are. While men are developing sensitivity to feelings at work, some of us still feel uncertain about bringing feelings into discussions with our male colleagues and mentors. As Debbie did with her male mentors, we maintain a focus-on-work approach. We choose to protect ourselves from having our feelings dismissed or taken as signs of weakness or uncertainty. We are comfortable saying that a new assignment is challenging or that we are excited about an opportunity. But we might withhold our ambivalence about how that challenge affects our esteem or what impact it may have on the people in our work group or family. Your women mentors will not be confused by or uncomfortable with these feelings. Instead, they will be inclined to read your feelings as expressions of authenticity, strength, and determination. With women you can be yourself. And when other women acknowledge your wholeness, you will emerge from your conversations feeling confident and powerful.

Women Know the Waters

The argument for having a female mentor, or mentors, gains dimension from Hermania Ibarra of the Harvard Business School. According to an article in the March 25, 1996 issue of *U.S. News & Word Report*, Ibarra studied four Fortune 55 corporations and found that women who were identified by their companies as being on the fast track had established connections with female as well as male mentors. "The high-potential women," Ibarra found, "were getting very concrete, gender-related career advice from the senior women that they just didn't get from men."

Catalyst, a nonprofit organization in New York that works to advance women in business, states in its publication "Perspective: A Case for Mentoring Women" that:

> clearly mentoring relationships offer advantages for pro-teges and mentors. Extensive research shows that a fe-male mentor can facilitate a protege's advancement by serving as a role model, helping her cope with work/fam-ily conflicts and other gender-related barriers, champion-ing her skills and successes, and providing career guidance.

The gender-related realities that affect your workplace accom-plishments and your work/life satisfaction can be most authenti-cally learned from a woman. Directly or indirectly, a woman has been affected by the choices women must make and by attitudes toward women in the milieu where she works. She has been in the water and knows the pull of the currents and the tug of the tides.

Sheila Wellington, president of Catalyst, observed in a 1997 interview on National Public Radio that the majority of the elite women Catalyst has studied report two factors that were important for their success: "One, consistently exceeding performance expectations. And the other, finding a style with which male managers are comfortable." The *Wall Street Journal* report on the recent Glass Ceiling Commission supported what Catalyst has found. "The biggest obstacle women face," the *Journal* concluded, "is also the most intangible; men at the top feel uncomfortable beside them."

It is your woman mentor who, from observation and experience, can guide you in breaking down the residue of discomfort and unfamiliarity some men still experience when working with women. She will tell you about walking the tightrope between men's expectations for how women should behave and how we need to behave in order to express our talents and our ideas. She will give you an insider's reading on the male/female culture of your work situation, and offer you choices and support as you develop your own effective style.

Sarah, a project director for a division of a computer products company, expressed the fine line she has learned to walk in this way: "I know I need to be assertive to be credible, and I know that if I become too macho, I will lose that credibility because the men in the meeting will become uncomfortable. I will fail to make an impact because their attention will turn from my point or my idea to why I am not acting like a woman!" Sarah shares her frustrations, her humor, and her experience with her younger protégés, but she does not advise them to bury their assertiveness—or their compassion when they are real and present. Instead, she listens, affirms her protégés' frustrations, and responds with support and encouragement. She does not want them to compromise their strengths or their passions to fit a limiting perception of how a woman is supposed to behave. "The more comfortable we are being our honest and genuine selves," she believes, "the more confident we will be with women and men. And when we can focus on our performance in a culture that accepts and respects all people, we will contribute to making others comfortable with our talent and our leadership."

Your women mentors, the ones who have struggled with gender perceptions and expectations, are the ones who can guide you. They are the ones who have a committed interest in encouraging you to find and develop your individual strengths, free of gender constraints. They are the ones who will lead you into the awakening culture that respects individuals and honors good performance.

Women Can Help You Move Ahead

Having any mentor or mentors, male or female, will definitely give you a practical career advantage.

Numerous studies confirm that women who say they have mentors report greater career success and higher job satisfaction than women going it alone.

In a study for their book *Women, Mentors and Success*, Joan Jeruchim and Pat Shapiro found that of 106 businesswomen surveyed, 77 percent said that they had a mentor. Of the 23 percent without mentors, most felt that they would have advanced more quickly if they had had a mentor.

In the past, women believed that male mentors were the ones who could give the advice and entreé one needed in order to advance and women who provided the encouragement and moral support. Now many women have achieved the positions of influence that were once mostly controlled by men. They have the access and can provide you with opportunities for challenge and exposure that are important elements in the mentoring process.

If it is still true that "women advance to their positions based on proven performance, and men are promoted based on perceptions of their potential," it follows that the women ahead of you are excellent performers who have been recognized and rewarded for their accomplishments. In identifying with and learning from these successful women, you will benefit from their visibility and you will be seen as another outstanding performer. And just as important as access and challenge,

---

women are also able to offer the understanding and caring that will nurture your self-esteem and encourage you to achieve your visions.

Women Are in Place to Become Your Mentors

The women who will mentor you as advisers and advocates are on the next floor, down the hall, on the phone, or checking their E-mail in offices across the country. According to the U.S. Bureau of Statistics, women constitute 47 percent of the workforce. In 1990, six million women called themselves managers, and more women join those ranks every day.

The March 25, 1996, issue of *U.S. News and World Report* stated that in 1995, women held 45 percent of all managerial positions in the United States, up from 32 percent in 1983. Within Fortune 2000 companies, the percentage of senior vice presidents and executive vice presidents who were women rose from 17 percent in 1982 to 32 percent in 1992. Eighty-one percent of Fortune 500 companies now have at least one woman director, and almost 25 percent of lawyers and doctors are women. According to the second annual Catalyst Consensus of Women Corporate Officers and Top Earners, released in December 1997, three-quarters of Fortune 500 companies—76 percent—had women corporate officers. Top earners in Fortune 500 companies had doubled over the past two years, bringing the total to 61 women. Women made up 2.5 percent of the total of 2,458 top earners, up from just 29 women, or 1.2 percent, two years earlier.

The women you need as your mentors are in place. And they are willing to join with you in mutually beneficial learning relationships.

Women Are Willing to Be Your Learning Partners

Thanks to help from Mary Pebley, education director of the American Business Women's Association, I was able to conduct an informal survey of women's experience helping and/or mentoring women. Of the women business owners, department managers, engineers, vice presidents, and company presidents who answered my questions, 87 percent said that they had been helped by a woman, 44 percent said that they had women mentors (18 percent were unsure), and 50 percent said that they were mentoring another woman.

Korn/Ferry International reported in its "Decade of the Executive Woman" survey released in 1993 that a full 87.9 percent of women executives polled said that they were serving as a mentor to a lower-level woman. *Working Woman* magazine in its August 1994 issue reported that "women have come a long way in helping other women get ahead." The article cited a *Working Woman*/MCI poll, conducted by Gallup, of 561 full-time executive and professional women. According to the magazine's summary, women under age 35 are more likely to have mentors than their older counterparts (60 percent for the younger women versus 48 percent for the older women). The majority of these mentors, 56 percent, were women.

More and more women are in positions where they can provide valuable mentoring to other women, not only in established brokerage houses, high-tech companies, and law firms, but in new and growing ventures founded and staffed by women. Consider that today, according to the National Foundation for Women Business Owners and Dun & Bradstreet Information Services, we have in the United States 7.7 million women-owned businesses generating nearly $1.4 trillion in sales and employing 15.5 million people—35 percent more people than are employed by the Fortune 500 companies worldwide. Women-owned firms employ one in every four workers in the United States. "The current economic turnaround is woman-driven and women hire women for the most part," wrote A. David Solver for *The Wall Street Journal* on May 5, 1994. More than half of the three billion businesses formed in the United States in each of the years from 1989 to 1994 were started by women, he noted, and the workforce in those women-owned companies is typically two-thirds female. That means that many of you are already working for or will be hired at some point by a women-owned company.

The opportunities for finding women as teachers and mentors wherever you work are greater now than at any time in our workplace history. It is up to you to make the most of this advantage.

How You Can Use This Book to Learn From Women

Timing and circumstance prompted Debbie to enter into her mentoring connection with Anna. Some women, however, are reluctant to seek mentors. "Instead," Connie Glaser observed in her book *Swim With the Dolphins*, "they wait to be chosen. Or they often fall into mentoring relationships without fully understanding the concept."

You don't have to wait to be chosen by women who will be your mentors. This book will encourage and prepare you to take the initiative in forming learning connections with women—and to manage those relationships for your and your mentors' advantage. As you read, you will become familiar with the concept of mentoring from a woman's perspective. You will learn how to make the most of woman-to-woman connections for your own growth and for a rewarding future for women in corporate and professional life. Consider this book itself as a learning resource. Then use what you have learned to extend the connections among women committed to achievement and to one another.

- Use the stories and examples as models for your learning relationships.
- Use the inventories to help you learn about yourself and to prepare you for learning most effectively from the women who are waiting to teach you.
- Follow the how-to guides and checklists to initiate and manage rewarding learning relationships.
- Read this book from front to back to appreciate the broad scope of woman-to-woman learning connections, or go to the chapter that is most relevant to what you need right now.

- Share this book with a prospective learning partner or group to make the most of the learning opportunity.
- Use the suggested readings to learn more about subjects that relate to your needs and interests.

If You Want to Learn More

These books will give you insights into what women have encountered in their progress to succeed and how the presence of women is changing the way all people communicate and do business in our careers and professional lives.

Driscoll, Dawn-Marie, and Carol R. Goldberg. *Members of the Club: The Coming of Age of Executive Women* (New York: The Free Press, 1993).

Glasser, Connie, and Barbara Steinberg Smalley. *Swim With the Dolphins: How Women Can Succeed in Corporate America on Their Own Terms* (New York: Warner Books, 1995).

Heim, Pat, Ph.D. *Hardball for Women: Winning at the Game of Business* (New York: Plume, 1993).

Helgesen, Sally. *The Web of Inclusion* (New York: Currency Doubleday, 1995).

Reardon, Kathleen Kelley, Ph.D. *They Don't Get It, Do They? Communication in the Workplace—Closing the Gap Between Women and Men* (Boston: Little, Brown, 1995).

Rosener, Judy B. *America's Competitive Secret: Utilizing Women as a Management Strategy* (New York: Oxford University Press, 1995).

Tannen, Deborah, Ph.D. *You Just Don't Understand: Women and Men in Communication* (New York: William Morrow and Co., Inc., 1990).

CHAPTER 2

Confronting the Myths and Fears That Have Kept Women Apart

G IVEN ALL THE convincing evidence of how women can benefit from mentoring relationships with other women, why do some aspiring, motivated women still resist making the connection? I asked this question in focus groups and individual interviews across the country. Megan's situation is typical of the explanations I heard from conscientious women who were just beginning their careers.

Fear of Appearing Demanding, Needy, and Weak

MEGAN'S STORY

Megan is a student at the UCLA law school. A petite, bright, natural blond, Megan has a contained, confident manner that will serve her well with her legal colleagues and clients. I have known her since her undergraduate years at Cornell University, and I talked with her recently about her experiences and expectations for establishing learning connections with women as she begins her law career. Megan was fortunate to be selected as a law intern at a prestigious Los Angeles–based firm the summer between her second and third years. At the end of her internship, she accepted the firm's offer to join it as a full-time associate after graduation. During the summer, the interns were encouraged to get to know the firm's associates and partners, an invitation Megan pursued with enthusiasm. Approximately 18 percent of the office's eighty partners are women, and 40 percent of the associates are women. Carrolle, a senior associate up for partner, seemed to take an interest in Megan's work future with the firm. Carrolle found opportunities to share conversations with Megan and gave Megan her perspective on working at the firm. Megan and Carrolle also spent time discussing the balance between work and personal life. Though Megan certainly appreciates what seems to be a willingness on the part of the senior woman to reach out to her, Megan is concerned about how to interpret and proceed with the relationship. "If I ask too many questions," she wonders, "will I appear needy and as if I want to have my hand held?" Megan went on to tell me, "I have heard that women over forty often resent young women who act as if we are 'owed something' simply because we are women and they are women. I respect what she and the other female partners have achieved. I know they had to struggle to get where they are, and I respect that. I don't want to appear pushy and demanding. Especially, though, I don't want her to think I am weak and unprepared." Megan would like to have a connection with a woman at work. She believes that learning from a woman about being a woman in her firm would be a great advantage. Just beginning her career, Megan wants guidance in how her work commitments will fit with her more holistic life goals. She knows that more senior female attorneys could help her, but she is not sure how to initiate a more definite protégé/mentor connection—or if she even should! "What if my approach backfired, and she rejected me?" Megan asked. "Would I be worse off than if I had never sought her support and advice?"

The situation Megan described is not uncommon. Intelligent women know that they would benefit from learning connections with other women, but they are hesitant to initiate the relationship. Megan's reasons for avoiding a direct discussion of an acknowledged learning connection or a mentoring relationship stem from her concern that she might appear to Carrolle to be weak and needy if she presumed to ask for help. Megan assumes that she has a responsibility to maintain an image of confidence and competence and not to threaten what women have achieved by presenting herself as needy. For a senior woman who has striven to prove her competence and capability for high performance, a younger woman who acknowledges her insecurity may sound an alarm and mark herself as threatening and to be avoided at all costs. Having worked so hard to build an image, why would someone like Carrolle risk letting someone like Megan suggest to the world that maybe women aren't so sure about our place and our potential?

Megan's hesitancy to establish an identified learning connection with Carrolle may deny her an opportunity to benefit from a valuable relationship. She means to be considerate, but her reasons for holding back may well be ill-founded. Women today are more confident of their accomplishments and positions than ever before. In my experience talking with people for this book,

---

women do not see asking for coaching and guidance as a weakness. Rather, they accept the gesture as a compliment and appreciate that a motivated woman with potential has singled them out.

Megan does, from her perspective, face a personal conflict. How can she benefit from what she knows Carrolle can teach her without appearing weak and needy? The answer lies in Megan's understanding of and respect for the situation, herself, and Carrolle. She can say to Carrolle at the beginning that she has become informed about Carrolle's accomplishments and has respect for her achievements. Megan can make it clear that she is confident of her own potential but knows that she may be able to avoid mistakes and make significant contributions to the firm more quickly if she can bring her questions and observations to Carrolle for advice and discussion. Then, when she has lunch with Carrolle or stops by her office in the late afternoon, Megan will be prepared to present herself as assured and mature. She will have a focused point to which Carrolle can respond. Finally, Megan must be sure to provide Carrolle with feedback on the action she takes—and to thank Carrolle for her time.

The Myth That You Will Be Rejected

Suppose Megan decides that she can manage her approach to Carrolle in a way that will not make her appear weak and needy. Megan knows that she is going to be a good lawyer and can succeed on her own, but she also recognizes the advantages that having a woman mentor could provide for her career and life planning. She is determined to approach Carrolle and to be up front about the relationship she wants with this senior woman. But she hesitates once again. What if Carrolle says no? How will Megan, or how would you in a similar situation, respond to the rejection?

"I would feel so deflated and defeated if I approached a woman to learn from her and she refused me!" I first heard this concern when I brought women in their mid-twenties together for a focus group in Chicago. They represented computer information systems consultants, women in advertising and marketing, and a woman in nursing. They were all smart, well prepared, and committed to their careers. They all saw advantages to having a female guide and advocate, and they all worried about being rejected if they asked for special attention and help. Since that afternoon, I have heard women from their twenties to their fifties express this same inhibition.

Yes, having any request rejected can be painful. Having another person reject you, especially when that person is a woman with whom you feel a gender connection, can be especially difficult. A woman is supposed to be caring and extending, so if she says no to being your mentor, a common response is to conclude that she must really not like you or not think you are any good!

When you make the decision to initiate a learning connection with another woman, be clear with yourself that you are taking charge. First, assess the situational politics at work to understand how a commitment to you might affect this woman's image and opportunities. If her acknowledging a committed developmental relationship with you appears to offer no obvious problems, ask yourself if she has made any comments or gestures that would suggest

16

that she has noticed you and has been favorably impressed. If that too yields a yes, deciding to approach her would seem reasonable and appropriate.

However, as with any business request, she may have real business reasons for saying no. When you approach her with your request, be prepared to hear a yes, a qualified yes, or a no. Listen to her reasons and respect her position. If she says she cannot make the time commitment, accept that she is most likely being very honest. Hear her if she tells you that she is currently working with another person or other women and thinks she cannot give you the careful consideration you deserve—right now. Try to see if she anticipates that you will be competing with her, and silently thank her for helping both of you avoid a potentially threatening situation if she is. The bottom line here is, don't feel that if she says she cannot at this time commit to a identified learning relationship, she is rejecting *you* as a person.

Chances are, however, that the woman you approach will be willing to help. Most women report that they are amenable to guiding and mentoring other women. She may limit the time and commitment she can offer you because of her own needs and goals, but a partial yes is not a rejection. If she does say no, she probably will still be honored that you admired her enough to approach her as mentor. When the time is right, she may come back and find you! And if you truly admire her and want to learn how she has succeeded in her position, you still have the option of observing her as a model. Finally, on the minimal chance that a woman says no, she may be doing you a great favor. If she feels the match isn't right— for her and for you—she has done you a great service by being honest and encouraging you to find someone with whom the connection will be solid and the rewards mutually beneficial.

Fear of being rejected by a woman you have sought as a mentor is not a good reason to lose a potential golden opportunity. Put yourself in control of the situation. Understand your position and hers, don't take a negative response personally if it comes, and continue to observe and learn from women you admire. Watch for the signs that a fit with another woman is right, and try again! The rewards are worth the waiting.

The Myth That Women "Owe You Something"

The opposite of a woman who fears being rejected is the woman who assumes that she has the right to be mentored. Kimberly sees herself as bright, well educated, and committed to rising to the top. For these reasons, she believes that women at the communications company where she works are obligated to help her accomplish her goals. After all, her success will reflect well on all women, and any woman would be doing sisterhood a service by rallying around her rising star.

Rather than attracting a line of willing mentors, Kimberly's disrespectful, self-centered demeanor has the effect of driving otherwise willing and generous women away and leaving the demanding would-be protégé isolated and confused. Women like Megan will find or be found by their mentors. Megans are respectful, appreciative, and open to learning. It is the women who are unlike Megan, the women like Kimberly who think they know it all already or who demand to be mentored, who will not benefit from the gifts women are prepared and positioned to offer.

Sandra Dijkstra, literary agent to Amy Tan, Susan Faludi, and many other big authors, has had numerous talented women working in her office. Sandy mentors primarily by doing her own job well and setting an example, but also by giving her employees a wide range of responsibilities. However, she does "work with and actively encourage the development of certain skilled employees, with a view toward their assuming greater responsibility in the company, which then widens their skills." "The heartbreak of mentoring," as Sandy sees it, is that, "too often young people believe they have to move on in order to grow rather than move up within the company that trained them."

Though these young people are not directly rejecting a woman

18

who mentored them, they have ended the connection before it could grow into a richer and deeper learning exchange. In this scenario, a valuable relationship has ended and both women may regret the loss. I have spoken to women in similar situations who admit that they resent having committed time, expertise, and caring to a young person who leaves the company prematurely. These women feel they have been burned and are reluctant to reach out to another young protégé. A protégé who has left for what she sees as growth opportunities outside the company may find it difficult to build trust with a new mentor. Though you may move on for healthy career reasons of your own, a new mentor may be reluctant to commit herself fully to a new learning relationship that could end the minute you see a better opportuninty across the street.

Rejecting mentors can exclude you from the valuable network of influential women. Demanding to be mentored can have a similar effect. Mary is a researcher, author, and professor in the Boston area. When she attended a symposium at a women's studies institute, she was distressed to encounter a panel of young women who demanded to be mentored by high achieving women in their career areas. Their attitude was, "You owe me something because I am a woman." Mary and her colleagues were reluctant to take on these would-be protégés who were so self-focused that there seemed little opportunity for good feeling or mutual benefit in the connection. Something you demand is not a gift. There are women who will withhold what they could share if they feel they are being used for their accomplishments rather than appreciated for their abilities and recognized for the dedication and the struggle that led to their achievements.

The Myth of the "Dead Even" Rule

The emphasis some women put on finding common ground with other women and denying differences can keep them apart from women who have experienced more, accomplished more, or advanced further than they have at a given point in their careers and their lives. Writers including Deborah Tannen, Ph.D., observe that often a woman is more comfortable with another woman when she can relate to ways in which they are alike instead of having to acknowledge differences, especially differences in position within a hierarchy. One of the functions of "rapport" talks between women, Tannen says, is to establish ways in which we are similar to, or peer with, another woman.

Anne Wilson Schaef, psychotherapist and writer, tells us in her touchstone book, *Women's Reality,* that when men come together at school, on the playing field, or at work, "the assumption is that one of them must be superior and the other must be inferior." Many men, research shows us, spend their social and working lives measuring and vying for who is one up or one down. In the female system, however, Schaef observes that "relationships are philosophically conceived as peer until proven otherwise." Familiarity with and acceptance of hierarchical relationships can make a mentor/protégé connection, with a leader and a learner, seem natural and normal. Many men come together easily and benefit from a hierarchical relationship.

This is not the case for those women who resist difference in position or power as the basis for a compatible connection with another woman. Dr. Pat Heim, former professor and now consultant and author of *Hardball for Women*, finds a negative effect for some women who emphasize sameness over respect for and acknowledgment of a woman's achievements in a workplace hierarchy. What she calls the "dead even rule" has women attacking and diminishing the achievements that put one woman ahead of another so that women can feel comfortable with their "sameness." Women with this level of discomfort with women "above" them will not be inclined to form positive learning connections with their female superiors.

If you are uncomfortable with differences of accomplishment in a connection with another woman, consider the potential for learning that you are denying yourself. Don't shoot yourself in the foot. Rather than seeing your different experience levels as a threat, consider your career choice and your dedication to learning and achieving to be the basis for your similarity. Respect what she knows and has experienced, and honor the wisdom she can share. Finally, honor the potential for mutuality in your learning connection with her. Though she may be ten years ahead of you or three levels above you, you have insights, talents, and skills that enter into the exchange. You will receive coaching and encouragement, and you can give back new ideas and support in exchange.

The Myth of the Queen Bee

You may understand the value of having a women as a coach, feedback resource, and advocate, but what if the model of success you admire turns out to be one of those dreaded Queen Bees? When Megan told me about Carrolle, she expressed the concern some women still experience when they consider reaching up to senior women, especially women age 40 or older. Though Carrolle seemed to be the one initiating the connection with Megan, Megan worried that if she were to suggest a more specific learning connection, Carrolle might become defensive and want to keep Megan out of the turf and territory she commanded. It may not happen often, but the myth persists that if you unwittingly get too close to a Queen Bee, she will attack, and her sting will poison you forever.

"Queen Bees," as Dr. Robin Ely of Columbia University describes them, were the "token women in traditionally male-dominated settings whom male colleagues rewarded for denigrating other women and for actively working to keep other women from joining them." They were the women who had staked out their territory and became defensive and protective if any other woman came close. They did exist, and there may still be one or two holed up in their hives. In all my interviews for this book, however, I met only a few woman who might fit the old profile, and not one of those woman had any interest in destroying would-be protégés. Rather, they were extremely busy, protective of their time and energy, and resentful of women who imposed on them with demands for special attentions they had never encouraged.

Karla, for example, may have taken on the form of a Queen Bee for Jamie when she said no to Jamie's request for monthly meetings and coaching sessions. "I had never even met this Jamie woman," Karla told me. "She called me because she was aware of my position in the division and thought I could do her some favors. I resented her assumptions and her lack of respect for my time and my work priorities. I might have been a bit brusque in denying her request, but she was wrong in approaching me that way." For Jamie, Karla may have come off as a Queen Bee. In fact, Karla has in many instances provided coaching and encouragement for promising women in her area. She takes her responsibilities as a boss to include coaching and developing the women and men she manages. Giving time to Jamie would, in Karla's mind, be taking time away from developing people on projects that benefited her bottom line—and reflected positively on her own performance. If Jamie had taken the time to learn about Karla and to respect Karla's position and obligations, she might have discovered not a Queen Bee, but a strong woman with clear priorities and a respect for herself and her performance obligations.

The myth of the Queen Bee should not be a reason for you to avoid respectfully approaching a woman you admire for short-term advice and feedback, or even for a more long-term learning relationship. Consider the information that comes from the Korn/Ferry "Decade of the Executive Woman" survey released in 1993. Though only 15 percent of the women executives surveyed for the report said that they had a woman mentor, 87.9 percent said that they were serving as a mentor to a lower-level woman. And my experience tells me that of the remaining women who were not actively mentoring, most would respond positively if you were to initiate a learning connection. Queen Bees are the exception, not the rule. Fear of a Queen Bee is no reason to avoid women who have the capacity and the willingness to assist you in developing your career.

The Myth of the Destructive Woman and Other Women-Can't-Work-With-Women Stereotypes

The Queen Bee wants to be the only female ruling her territory. She isn't encouraging or friendly to other women, identifies herself with men, and puts women down whenever she has the opportunity. She is a very specific type who wants to isolate and detach herself from any pressure to develop and promote other women.

She is not, however, the only type of woman that women fear encountering in the workplace. Myths also exist that tell us that women can't work with women, that women are duplicitous, back-biting gossips whose advice or confidences can't be trusted. The myth sets up women as nasty, destructive competitors, just waiting for an opportunity to betray or sabotage you if you appear to be moving ahead.

Ever since my 1993 book on woman-to-woman working relationships, *When Women Work Together: Using Our Strengths to Overcome Our Challenges*, the Destructive Woman has hovered as a ugly specter during my workshops and conference talks. Women in these sessions ask, "How can I trust a woman to be honest and give me direction and support, when I know how badly women treat each other at work?"

My first response to these questions is to tell these women not to assume the worst but to let women prove themselves first. We do a serious disservice to ourselves and to the women with whom we could form valuable learning relationships when we distance ourselves from women because of the persistence of these overblown stereotypes.

I am convinced that some of the negative rap women have heard about other women comes from our confused expectations concerning the ways in which women relate to one another at home and in our communities and how we must conduct ourselves if we are to be honest, healthy, effective business and professional people.

Our female gender culture has prepared us to have high expectations for other women to be caring, considerate, and friendly, and to put "relationship" and cooperation first.

When reasonable workplace situations make us appear more critical than caring, we are not being cruel saboteurs.

When during a period of stress we seem more devoted to production and the bottom line than to the emotional needs of our colleagues, we have not become cold, destructive women. Rather, we are behaving as responsible women functioning in a workplace that demands performance. If we sometimes come across as "not nice" when we have to be direct about our needs and selective about who can deliver and who cannot, we are not being Destructive Women. We do not deserve to be punished by other women who demand that we consider their feelings first. When we respond with fairness and honesty to the demands of a functional workplace, we are demonstrating our ability to act and deliver. We are still good women. We are at work, and we are doing a good job.

Dr. Judith Briles is one of a group of researchers and writers who have studied women's behavior toward women at work. Although her major theme is that women behave unethically toward women at work and that the instances of sabotage increased between her first study in 1987 and her follow-up study in 1993, her statistics report some positive news as well. In her 1994 book, *The Briles Report on Women in Health Care*, she reported that 88 percent of the women she studied said that they had been actively helped by women. My work and experience tell me that women are more likely to be positive than negative about their working experiences with other women. On open-ended surveys, over and over again they tell me that they appreciate women's willingness to extend to others and connect on a personal level, their caring, their competence, and their willingness to cooperate. In *When Women Work Together*, I refer to these areas as women's four comfort zones: connection, caring, competence, and cooperation.

24

Other information that may help allay a fear of the Destructive Woman stereotype comes from Dr. Robin Ely's article "The Effects of Organizational Demographics and Social Identity on Relationships Among Professional Women," published in the *Administrative Quarterly* in 1994. Ely has studied women lawyers in firms in which few women hold senior positions and in firms in which women are well represented at the senior, partner level. She has concluded that when women are well represented at senior levels, junior women are less competitive with one another and generally have positive experiences with their woman-to-woman working relationships. "Women's proportional representation in senior positions of an organization," Ely wrote, "may signal to junior women the extent to which positions of power are attainable by women."

Ely went on to write that:

When women perceive that the boundary to top positions is permeable, and it is credibly so, their gender identity is less likely to create problems, because they are less likely to perceive their sex as incompatible with success and promotion. Rather than presenting a dilemma, senior women in these sex-integrated organizations are likely to represent to junior women evidence of women's capacity to succeed, and identifying with women is likely to be a positive experience. Able to draw on shared gender, as well as benefit from differences in experience, knowledge, and skill, junior women are more likely to construct satisfying developmental relationships with their senior women counterparts.

Megan's, for example, belongs in the category of organizations in which the expectation for positive woman-to-woman relationships follows the proportion of women in senior position. Megan so far has experienced welcoming, sharing connections with the women associates and with other women interns, close to half of the summer group. The current 18 percent of women at the partner level

25

appear to be accessible to the junior women and to encourage them rather than plot to destroy their success.

I predict that as women continue to move into positions of visibility and power within their organizations and professions, the old rule that "the oppressed destroy each other" will no longer apply to women, and the Destructive Woman will follow the Queen Bee into extinction.

When you look for constructive learning relationships with women at work, expect to find women who will be willing to help and support you. Don't let the myth of the Destructive Woman keep you from reaching out and establishing connections with colleagues and senior women who can be your sounding boards, guides, and advocates. However, be alert and astute. If you know that a woman—or a man—has a reputation for unethical or do-others-in behavior, keep your distance. Expect the best from other people, but don't be a fool.

Taking Your Pulse on Woman-to-Woman Relationships

You know that you can benefit from forming constructive, supportive relationships with other women at work. The evidence presented in this book so far, I hope, has convinced you of that. You have confronted the factors that may have kept you from reaching out to women who can help you achieve your professional and career goals, and you are ready to avail yourself of a golden opportunity—learning from women. However, you may hesitate because of your own personal biases. Even in the face of reasonable arguments that favor what women have achieved and what women can offer, you aren't really convinced, at a gut level, of women's value and trustworthiness. Until you understand yourself and your attitudes toward women, and until you can work with those beliefs that inhibit your confidence in women, you will not be able to realize the full benefits of woman-to-woman learning opportunities. As a first step in preparing yourself to be receptive to what other women can offer for your career and your life, please take the following inventory. Answer the questions honestly—what you feel, not what you believe you should think. Mark one of the three possible responses, or simply use the questions to focus your reflections on your woman-to-woman experiences and expectations. If personal biases are keeping you from reaching out to women as supports and mentors, this inventory can be the first step in helping you past the impediments and allowing you to benefit from the rewards of positive, woman-to-woman learning experiences.

Inventory	Agree	Not Sure	Disagree
1. If I could choose, I would prefer to work for a woman rather than a man.	❐	❐	❐
2. I have no preference as to working with a woman or a man.	❐	❐	❐
3. I have close women friends.	❐	❐	❐
4. In general, I would say that my relationships with women are good.	❐	❐	❐
5. I look forward to meeting and working with women.	❐	❐	❐
6. I assume another woman to be as competent as a man in the same position.	❐	❐	❐
7. I believe women are as capable as men of holding the highest-level management/ professional positions.	❐	❐	❐
8. I expect a woman to work as hard as, if not harder than, a man.	❐	❐	❐

Inventory	Agree	Not Sure	Disagree
9. I have had positive working relationships with women in the past.	❏	❏	❏
10. I expect that a woman will acknowledge and reward my good work.	❏	❏	❏
11. I believe that support from women can help my career success.	❏	❏	❏
12. I have identified women who serve as models for how I want to manage my career and myself.	❏	❏	❏
13. I have had positive experiences with women in positions of responsibility and authority.	❏	❏	❏
14. I believe a woman mentor can offer me useful insights and instruction.	❏	❏	❏
15. I have benefited from women who have coached or advised me.	❏	❏	❏
16. I have had a woman, or women, advocate for me.	❏	❏	❏
17. I would seek the opportunity to be mentored by a woman.	❏	❏	❏

If you tend to agree with the statements in the inventory, then you are well positioned to be receptive to options for reaching up, reaching out, and learning from women. Your positive attitude toward senior women and female coworkers will provide an excellent base for what these women can teach you. Also, your positive expectations concerning women's place and accomplishments at work will prompt you to welcome women as promoters of your talents and potential when you or they identify opportunities that will benefit your goals. If the inventory shows you that you are not sure or that you often disagree with the statements about women, then I suggest you explore your reasons for these responses. Have you had actual experiences to support your answers, or are you reacting to old stories and stereotypes that have sometimes put women in a dismal light as coworkers and bosses? If experience has been your teacher, is it right to generalize this to all women, or can you revisit the situation and see it as an isolated case with an unfortunate person? If you are reflecting stereotypical notions, reconsider the fears and myths in this chapter and be willing to make new woman-to-woman connections and consider them in a new light.

Women in your careers and professions offer gold to be mined. Be prepared, take the initiative, and enjoy the rich rewards.

If You Want to Learn More

For more background on woman-to-woman workplace relationships, with examples and solutions, I suggest you look at the following books. For an interesting take on protégés doing their mentors in, consider renting *All About Eve,* the 1950 movie with Bette Davis and Anne Baxter. Then, of course, while you're there pick up *Working Girl* with Sigourney Weaver and Melanie Griffith!

Barber, Jill, and Rita E. Watson. *Sisterhood Betrayed: Women in the Workplace and the All About Eve Complex* (New York: St. Martin's Press, 1991).

Briles, Judith. *The Briles Report on Women in Health Care: Changing Conflict to Collaboration in a Toxic Workplace* (San Francisco: Jossey-Bass Publishers, 1994).

Duff, Carolyn, and Barbara Cohen. *When Women Work With Women: Using Our Strengths to Overcome Our Challenges* (Berkeley, Calif.: Conari Press, 1993).

CHAPTER 3

A Woman's Way of Mentoring: Entering the Gift Exchange

ONCE YOU HAVE put behind you any concerns about initiating or accepting a mentoring connection with another woman, what can you expect the learning experience to be like? How might women be advancing and extending the concept of mentoring as we give to each other in our careers and in our lives?

JAN AND BETTY

Jan stood behind the podium, ready to introduce the keynote speaker. At the head table, Betty Stallings, a tastefully dressed, attractive woman in her early fifties, shuffled her note cards, then smiled up at Jan. As a nationally acclaimed presenter and thirteen-year executive director of the Valley Volunteer Center in Pleasanton, California, Betty was often invited to speak at meetings and conferences. This day she was close to home, and she knew Jan, the conference chair, because of Jan's position as coordinator of volunteers at a large local hospital.

"And now," Betty heard Jan say, "I present Betty Stallings, my mentor, and mentor to many women who have known and worked with her over the years."

Jan's description stunned Betty, and she hesitated for a moment before moving to the podium. Mentor? Betty understood how she might have been a model for Jan, someone Jan observed from a distance. That was not, however, the sort of learning connection and advocacy role that Betty associated with "mentor." "If I'd only known she saw me as a mentor," Betty admonished herself, "I could have offered her so much more!"

What Betty would have offered Jan earlier and what the two are experiencing today is a holistic, growing relationship based on mutual respect and focused on career development and whole-life integration. Both women are benefiting from mentoring the female way.

Progressing From the Male Mentoring Tradition

Mentor is a character in Homer's *Odyssey*. In Homer, Mentor was teacher and guide to Ulysses' son Telemachus as Ulysses wended his way home from the Trojan War. From Mentor's example evolved the concept of mentoring, or acting like Mentor. A mentor acts as coach, critic, adviser, counselor, model, and guide, sometimes playing all the parts, other times emphasizing one function over another. Also, a mentor is assumed to act as an advocate, or champion, who works to create opportunities and advantages for a favored protégé. The mentor may include character development in the training process, but the success of traditional mentoring is measured in terms of advancement, salary increases, and positional power.

Kathy Kram, in her thorough and touchstone book *Mentoring at Work: Developmental Relationships in Organizational Life,* looked at mentoring as a structured relationship between an experienced person and a person wanting to learn from the more experienced senior. She defined mentoring as a hierarchical relationship incorporating two types of functions: career functions and psychosocial functions. The career functions include:

(1) Sponsorship
(2) Exposure and viability
(3) Coaching

(4) Protection
(5) Challenging assignments

The psychosocial functions include:

(1) Role modeling
(2) Acceptance and confirmation
(3) Counseling
(4) Friendship

"When a hierarchical relationship provides all of these functions," she observed, "it best approximates the prototype of a mentor relationship."

A brochure announcing a corporate-sponsored mentoring program for women at a financial products company provides a three-part definition of a mentor: (1) An established businessperson who gives advice and guidance to a client/protégé; (2) one who helps the client/protégé to develop, both personally and professionally; and (3) one who can enhance the sense of completeness and confidence of the client/protégé.

The tenets of the traditional mentoring model seem clear and consistent. The mentoring activities serve the function of developing new people to fill the ranks, to take over positions on the battlefield or in the organization.

Traditional mentoring provides well-trained and adapted followers to fill functional positions in the style of the mentor who delivered the coaching and advocated for the formative opportunities.

Though Mentor in Homer's story was a male guiding and counseling another male, in fact Mentor had a guide himself, Minerva, or Athena, goddess of wisdom. It was she, a female, who took Mentor's form and served as sidekick and adviser to the young Telemachus. It is interesting to wonder how the relationship might have played out if Athena had acted in her own gender as adviser to a young female. Would the ground for the connection have been different? Would the goals have been different? Would the style or the method of developing the junior person have had a different character, a different tone?

What potentially distinguishes woman-to-woman mentoring from traditional hierarchical man-to-man and man-to-woman mentoring is based on our female identity and culture. When we can express ourselves as women with women in a workplace learning connection, we will discover a release of potential that only being genuine can engender.

Our woman-to-woman learning relationships will put more emphasis on collaboration than on hierarchy, more on exchanging gifts than on bestowing wisdom. The scope of our learning experiences will be broad-based, not limited to career or professional function. Caring, committed woman-to-woman mentoring will consider the wholeness of a woman's life, a life that includes work, family, love, community, and spiritual well being. The potential for this new form exists with every woman now looking for a mentor and for every woman ready and willing to be a mentor.

New Dimensions for Woman-to-Woman Mentoring

"Mentoring," Jean Yancy told me as I talked with her in her Denver room, books and a newspaper on her bed, flowers from a friend aging in a glass vase, "is a cold, glacial word." Jean herself is the antithesis of cold. She is a warm, generous woman in her eighties who has been mentor, guide, friend, and advocate to scores of women. To celebrate Jean's encouraging friendship, three hundred Denver women collected funds for her 80th birthday and dedicated a bench at Cherry Creek State Park in her honor. Jean's bench is a symbol of the time she has taken to listen, care, and guide women who have come to her for direction.

For Jean, the word *mentoring* in its traditional sense does not say enough. "It is," she says with a smile, "wrong." Mentoring, from Jean's experience, suggests something "too objective, too intentional, too structured, and cold." Friendship—true, giving friendship—seems to Jean to come closer to describing what happens when one woman provides caring, guidance, and encouragement to another. "In the old male way, mentoring means having a plan for someone," Jean explained. "When I help someone, I don't have a plan for what I want this woman to become. What I do is see more ability, more strength in her than she sees in herself, and I help her discover herself."

A woman's way of mentoring, Jean's way, develops not a product but a person; not a performance but a confident performer who discovers new horizons for her potential and is encouraged to reach and to excel.

Karen Wedge, director of women's programs and studies at Colorado State University, seconds Jean's concern about the cold, limiting connotations of "mentoring" when the term is applied to the rich potential in woman-to-woman learning experiences. "Women who try to mentor or to be mentored in the traditional male hierarchical style generally do not find satisfaction in the relationship," Karen stated emphatically. "Mentoring for women is a process that happens to us; it is a gift exchange."

Sue Curry Jansen supports Yancy and Wedge's observations and concerns. In her article "What Is Mentoring? Some Feminist Digs," Jansen explored ideas for a new female mentoring model. She looked back to Robin Morgan and *Sisterhood Is Powerful* for another consideration of the male model. Morgan, Jansen wrote, embraced the idea of "sisterhood." "She rejected the surrogate father role Mentor played in instructing Telemachus," she continued. "Instead she used the metaphor of sisterhood to describe feminist women teaching, learning, advising, networking, laughing, crying, struggling and discovering solidarity together."

A group of women I visited at AT&T in New Jersey were spending hours of meeting time grappling with what to call their inchoate support program for women. They also rejected *mentoring* as too male, too prescribed. After several months, they agreed to call their activity "fostering."

Fostering is a term that frequently comes up when women probe the meaning and potential of woman-to-woman learning connections. I had a conversation about mentoring and fostering with Stephanie Strickland. Stephanie developed the women's studies collection at Sarah Lawrence College Library and recently won two distinguished awards for her new book of poems, *True North*. "In a professional field," Stephanie says, "a mentor is someone who helps a younger person to learn the unspoken and provides information beyond the expected."

As a poet, Stephanie prefers to use the word *fostering* to describe what happens among women artists. Fostering lets the woman know that where she is is fine and that she can go forward. Fostering, Stephanie says, is enabling, whereas mentoring is an activity that can be "business-oriented and hard-edged." "Fostering is building the person, the poet; mentoring is giving opportunities, getting the manuscript to the right editor. A woman mentors when she has power and can provide advantage; she fosters when she cares about another's vision and encourages her to realize her vision."

Stephanie uses *mentoring* and *fostering* to describe two distinctly different learning relationships. From what I have observed in my own relationships and in the learning relationships of women I have interviewed, woman-to-woman mentoring encompasses the benefits and values of both mentoring, in the traditional sense, and fostering. Women as mentors provide coaching, information, and opportunity. We also encourage a vision and support another woman's growth and worth.

I have tried to find or invent a new word to describe what happens when women learn from, encourage, and support each other in a work and life context. One writer who interviewed me for an article on workplace mentoring preferred to use "womentoring" when referring to female mentoring pairs. To me that seems contrived and potentially limiting. Mentoring between women should not become subject to specific rules and expectations. It should be a dynamic, organic exchange that grows in possibility as the individuals and their relationship grow. Rather than inventing a new word to distinguish woman-to-woman mentoring, I prefer that we put our emphasis on the substance and spirit of the connection as we experience it. Mentoring between women encompasses all the encouragement, wisdom, and support that we can give.

The Essence of Woman-to-Woman Mentoring Connections

Women have always learned from women. We have learned by watching and being guided by our mothers, our grandmothers, our aunts, teachers, coaches, counselors, professors, sisters, and friends. We have studied in the kitchens and gardens of women with degrees in living. Through stories and example, by answering our questions and nudging us with their own, women have passed on to other women lessons in how to live. More specifically, they have taught us how to recognize, understand, and respect ourselves as rich, complex female beings.

Today the potential to continue learning from women is also available to you in a workplace context. You will discover in many of these woman-to-woman connections ways of relating, sharing, and learning that reflect mentoring from a female perspective. Women are bringing to the tradition of training and advocating a female tone, a female value structure, a female style, and a female strength.

Relationship: The Foundation of Woman-to-Woman Mentoring

In woman-to-woman mentoring, the connecting that takes place often involves all the complexities of intimacy that characterize female relationships. As women, we are drawn to other women because we find someone we like, with whom we can be ourselves. It would be unusual for women in a mentoring pair not to like and want to know each other. Many women will extend to others by exchanging personal as well as work-related information. Through our talk we offer gifts of intimacy to another woman. We discover whether we like her and decide whether she likes us.

For many women I have interviewed, the mentoring connection feels less like a workplace function and more like a friendship based on affinity and respect. Anne Wilson Schaef, in *A Woman's Reality*, distinguished involvements that work for men and involvements that describe female relationships. Men find "buddies" or "pals" who can be relied upon to support the team effort. Often their interactions focus on an activity, such as their work or sports, that is outside themselves. Thus, the male mentoring connections focus on developing skills and strategies that support performance on the workplace battlefield or playground. For women, Schaef explained, "the focus of friendship is verbal intimacy and the mutual sharing of one's being. True friends are those who totally expose themselves to each other, sure in the knowledge that to do so is safe."

The bonding that comes from shared intimacy can be a powerful foundation for valuable learning and commitment. However, the intricacies involved in managing how deeply and in what ways we want to know and be known by another woman at work can complicate the relationship and even destroy it if we are not aware of the emotional factors and do not manage them to support, not threaten, the learning objective. (You can read more about managing these challenges in Chapter 6.) The strength in caring and sharing builds the bonds that will make woman-to-woman mentoring a powerful force for connecting women to women in the evolving future workplace.

Goals for Mentoring in the Female Form

At a coffee shop in Cambridge on a bright fall afternoon, I met with Dr. Eleanor Hobbs, who at the time was chief of emergency medicine at Deaconess Hospital in Boston. Dr. Hobbs is involved with the Radcliffe College mentor program and has mentored both men and women in the medical profession. I asked her if she could distinguish a female mentoring style from a male style. Though Dr. Hobbs was reluctant to generalize for all women or all men, she was willing to speak from her own experience and from what she has observed with her colleagues. "Through the mentoring activity," she explained to me, "a man justifies his own life. A man picks a protégé and tries to model that protégé after himself. I have noticed that my approach to mentoring is not so much that a protégé can justify my life as that she or he can find the life that is right for him or for her."

Current research confirms that men are more inclined to define themselves by their professional roles than are women. Women have a broader base of defining ourselves. We don't split ourselves into separate component parts. As a result, we have a harder time segmenting our lives. At all times, I am a business owner, a writer, a mother, a wife, a daughter. When I mentor another woman, I perceive her to be a person with many intertwined roles, responsibilities, and goals.

Women intuitively understand this blending of selves and bring this holistic view to our roles as mentors. Dr. Hobbs and many women I have subsequently interviewed have told me that their first obligation in mentoring women—and men—is to the whole person, not to the company or the profession. If Dr. Hobbs were mentoring a new emergency room doctor and the fit did not seem right for the individual, she would not feel a need to create a clone to justify her own career choice. Maria Vilar, a partner at Deloitte + Touche, LPP, in San Diego, made it very clear to me that when she mentors young women, she does not hesitate to suggest another company or even another profession if that seems best for the person, the whole person, she is mentoring.

This approach was echoed by Peg Pashkow, former vice president of rehabilitation services at Heather Hill, Inc., in Cleveland, Ohio. Peg was responsible for all of the clinical services at this progressive rehabilitation hospital and has had opportunities to mentor many women, individually and as members of her staff. "It is essential for successful mentoring that people consider the person and not just that person's function or role," she explained. "The functions of a person can change or be eliminated, but the person continues to develop and grow."

In most cases, your woman-to-woman mentoring relationship will be built on knowing, being known, and caring. Your mentor will respond to the multiple aspects of your life and guide you toward what is most appropriate and most fulfilling for you.

Mutual Learning as a Gift Exchange

I had asked Christine to meet me for lunch so that I could talk to her about her experience with mentors. Christine has a varied background that includes a master's degree from Harvard and work as a computer store owner, wellness newsletter editor, marketing manager for a Fortune 100 corporation, medical writer, and director for a New York high-tech communications company. We had been chatting about the subject of mentors when Christine surprised me by saying, "Let's talk about our relationship. You are my mentor!"

Christine had worked for me on a major writing/editing project, and we had kept in touch, meeting for coffee and long, rapid fire conversations covering our various endeavors and community connections. I was always interested in Christine's activities, and our relationship had spanned her ventures as a contract writer and a project manager and her decision to leave both her job and her worn-out marriage. She would talk, I would listen and question, we would talk more, and sometimes I would have observations that helped her frame her actions and decisions.

Basically an assured and certainly a multicapable person, Christine could sometimes let her assertive personality steamroll people in her path. When her stridency eroded friendliness and relationships suffered, her confidence collapsed and she lost sight of her strengths. We would discuss control issues and come up with new strategies to help her balance relationship management with performance demands.

Although I am ten years older than Christine and she had once worked for me, I did not consider myself her mentor. Rather, I was learning from Christine about the politics and working style of her high-tech company. I was also learning from her about risk and assertiveness, two areas where she had much greater experience—and success— than I.

Also, Christine became a motivator and supporter of my first book. Informally, I would run ideas by her and she would comment, adding anecdotes from her experience and troubleshooting solutions to the scenarios we discussed. When I flagged, she prodded. When I despaired, she cheered. And her encouragements were not hollow. We had written and edited together. She knew the frustrations, and she was convinced that I could and should persevere to the finish.

If I was Christine's mentor, she was also mine. It did not matter that our careers took different directions. We offered each other an understanding sounding board, insight from our experiences, coaching, guidance, and encouragement based on belief in each other's abilities and respect for our commitments. We helped each other see ourselves as better than we had previously seen ourselves, and we encouraged each other to move ahead on that offered confidence. Even though I was married with growing children and she was about to leave a marriage with no children, we found similarity in our appreciation of challenge, good work, strong values, and the power and satisfaction that come from reaching out and offering another support and affirmation.

That day, as we enjoyed our chicken tarragon salads, I realized that our learning connection, our mentoring relationship mirrored what I had been hearing from other women I had interviewed across the country. Sometimes we are too close to our own situations to see the pattern. Though, in a sense, a hierarchy of age and employer/employee framed our relationship, our learning was mutual and reciprocal. We both gave and received gifts of insight

41

and encouragement. From our respect grew trust and a vested caring in the other's accomplishments.

Also, the ways in which we coached and guided each other were distinctly female in tone and intention. We could empathize with each other, put ourselves in the other's place. Where men have been identified by researchers as "separate knowers"—individuals who can approach knowledge objectively and reduce it to understandable parts—women tend to be "connected knowers."

Women make sense of reality by relating new knowledge to experience in the context of relationships.

Often the stories women tell to increase information are stories of relationships, stories that might frustrate some male learners who want only the "facts."

We should not be surprised to hear again that many women value learning from others, and that more men than women find greater advantage in learning from activities and challenges than from other people. In a study of junior and senior high math students in a Colorado school district, girls reported that they preferred to work in groups rather than solve problems alone. Boys preferred to go solo on the challenging assignments. In their updated study on how women gain experience in their careers, Sharon Rogolsky and Maxine Dalton of the Center for Creative Leadership reported that women executives attribute 23.5 percent of their important developmental experiences to learning from others as opposed to learning from assignments, challenges, or other lesson-providing experiences.

Christine and I learned from each other. We used personal anecdotes to humanize our criticism and deliver coaching lessons. We were saying, "I can make mistakes too, and this is what happened to me and this is how I recovered." Women aren't as hesitant to admit our imperfections and even our failures to another woman as men are to share their failures as a basis for coaching and building the skills of their protégés. From this openness can come true gifts from mentor to protégé, and from protégé to mentor, that nourish our growth.

Woman-to-woman mentoring allows for uncertainty as a fertile condition from which decision and action grow. Faith Popcorn, in her 1996 book *Clicking,* talked about what she calls "FemLogic." As Popcorn observed, many women find it comfortable and natural to approach our decision-making discussions with "what if" questions. We move through our explorations assuming that "if A equals B and B equals C, then A equals C, but that may change if it rains." For many women, the inconclusiveness of the "what if's" is not unsettling. Rather, "prowling" a situation or an opportunity in this way can seem more real than creating a linear sequence of causes and effects that never quite diagrams the many facets of the situation. When Christine and I evaluated possible career moves and strategies, though we had not read Popcorn's book, we definitely used the FemLogic formula.

My style for interacting with Christine and with other women who have considered me a mentor is not to lecture, not to pronounce and direct, but rather to suggest and to guide. The process in woman-to-woman mentoring is one of discovery. As the protégé discovers herself, her answers, and her strength, both she and her learning guide are rewarded.

An investment banker I met at a conference where I was speaker shared with me why being a mentor to an aspiring, enthusiastic protégé was for her such a rewarding experience.

> When Maya comes to me with questions about how to conduct this or that client meeting, or how to present herself for promotions, I want to give her the best response I can. That often means I have to go back and review decisions I have made, what I have done and how it worked or didn't work. I share this process with her, and together we discover the fabric underlying the pattern of my achievements. I can be open with her, exploring my own experience so that I can give her the truth. I

become stronger, knowing who I am. And she applies what we have discovered to her own situation and goals. She then makes her decisions based on what she has learned from me and about herself.

Within a woman-to-woman mentoring connection, you will discover yourself. Together you and your mentor will expand the circumference of mentoring to encompass the female form, in all its complexities and richness. You will create a relationship based on trust and respect, and you will share in the process of learning. From this authentic base you will build the skills and decide the actions that will enhance your career and enrich your life.

If You Want to Learn More

For in-depth background on mentoring in the organizational context, you will want to read:

Kram, Kathy. *Mentoring at Work: Developmental Relationships in Organizational Life*, (Lanham, Md.: University Press of America, Inc., 1988).

I also suggest you read:

Belenky, Mary Field, Blythe McVicker Clinchy, Nancy Rule Goldberger, and Jill Mattuck Tarule. *Women's Way of Knowing: The Development of Self, Voice, and Mind* (New York: Basic Books, 1986).
Huang, Al Ching-ling, and Jerry Lynch. *Mentoring: The Tao of Giving and Receiving Wisdom* (San Francisco: HarperSanFrancisco, 1995).
Murray, Margo, with Marna A. Owen. *Beyond the Myths and Magic of Mentoring: How to Facilitate an Effective Mentoring Program* (San Francisco: Jossey-Bass, 1991).
Popcorn, Faith. *Clicking* (New York: HarperCollins, 1996).
Zey, Michael. *The Mentor Connection: Strategic Alliances in Corporate Life* (New Brunswick, N.J.: Transaction Publishers, 1991).

CHAPTER 4

Recognizing the Gift: Five Forms of the Woman-to-Woman Mentoring Connection

I HOPE YOU appreciate the great potentials that lie in woman-to-woman mentoring relationships. You may, though, still be unsure of how the relationship will define itself or how comfortable you will be with the binds and blessings of the connection. Your first step is to be open and receptive to the gifts of a mentoring connection. After that, you have many options for the degree of informality or formality in the possibilities that present themselves. What is important is that you recognize the learning opportunities in your connections with other women, and that you pursue the gifts they offer.

KAIA AND DARCY

Kaia Histand, a twenty-six-year-old senior product design engineer with Nike, was facing her annual performance review. As part of the process, Kaia would be asked to evaluate her strengths and challenges and to identify her goals and future plans. After putting much thought into preparing for the review, Kaia decided to ask someone she respected to give her feedback on her performance and her plans for the future. The person she chose to approach was a woman, Darcy, who at that time was director of advanced research and development for Nike.

Darcy Winston had been manager of Kaia's footwear design group, and Kaia had admired her style and the quality of her work. They had traveled together on flights to Taiwan, sharing life stories and interweaving the values that directed their lives. Though Kaia was 26, was not married, and had no children, and Darcy was in her early forties with a teenage son, they developed a friendship based on spontaneous affinity.

The two women occasionally ran together, and when Darcy's husband was ill, Kaia contributed casserole dinners for the family. At work, Kaia sought out Darcy to answer her project-related questions. A trust grew between the older and younger women, a trust that encouraged Kaia to take a definitive step and ask Darcy if she would act as a sounding board as Kaia prepared for her review.

Kaia's approach was to send Darcy an informal E-mail, saying how much she had appreciated Darcy's counsel and guidance in the past and asking if she would now, please, consider talking with her about the upcoming review. Darcy responded enthusiastically to Kaia's inquiry. Their relationship as experienced leader and ambitious learner, or in traditional terms as mentor and protégé, has continued beyond that first performance review prep session. The connection they have established is, according to Kaia and Darcy, "not a formal thing." Both women feel more comfortable just letting their relationship happen, without labels and without any formal agenda.

The answer to why Kaia would seek a woman mentor came easily. "First," Kaia made clear, "I have worked with Darcy, and I know what kind of a person she is. I admire her performance and her style. She is a powerful woman with an attitude toward our position as females in a male-dominated environment that I respect. Darcy has confidence in her abilities and puts value on her work. She feels no need to rebel. She is not defensive about being a woman, and I like that."

What, I then asked, did Kaia expect from this learning connection, this mentorship, that perhaps she could not expect from one of her male mentors? Kaia was very clear that her choice of Darcy for this role was based first on Darcy's professionalism and her position in the company. Darcy was in an ideal position to see things from a top-down perspective, a perspective that could help Kaia make strategic choices in building her career. Second, Kaia appreciated that she would get information from

Darcy that no man could offer. She could talk with Darcy about opportunities and positioning, and she could also talk about the impact of her choices on the whole, balanced life she wants to live as a woman. "Darcy understands the woman things, the quality of life issues, the feelings about being a woman in a male-dominated business. She will coach me as a whole person, not simply as a good performer." Third, Kaia liked Darcy and respected her style and her values. If the third factor had not existed, if there had been no affinity between the two women, no matter how well positioned Darcy had been, Kaia would not have sought her counsel.

Kaia and Darcy have an informal, yet acknowledged mentoring connection. "It's a friendship with a business fringe," Kaia tries to explain, "Or, maybe, a business relationship with a friendship fringe."

Finding the Most Comfortable Fit

No one form of woman-to-woman learning/mentoring connection fits all people or all pairs. You know how comfortable you yourself are with degrees of formality in your relationships. You will also learn what connections are comfortable for women you admire and respect. The following five forms of the female learning connection come from interviews I have conducted with women over the past three years. You have many creative options in how you will pursue and acknowledge your learning relationships. In the following descriptions of women learning with women, you may identify your own preferences or recognize the comfort level of women with whom you are connected. You are never limited to one mentor or one style of mentoring. But you do limit yourself if you do not seek to make a connection and benefit from what women can give.

When You Say Mentor and She Says Friend

For some women, the most cherished and richest reward in woman-to-woman relationships is the gift of friendship. From the empathetic, caring connection of friendship come naturally the exchanges that nurture, develop, and encourage a woman to be her best. Anything less than friendship denies women the full range of possibilities in a learning connection. It is only in the context of friendship that some women feel comfortable giving and receiving lessons from another woman.

Barbara Grogan is president of Western Industrial Contractors. One day I was in a conference room at Western Industrial, drinking coffee and talking with Barbara about women seeking women as mentors. Many women look up to Barbara as an example of an independent, savvy, successful business leader. Women want to learn from Barbara, but Barbara resists identifying the relationships that develop as "mentoring." For Barbara, mentoring and friendship are inextricably entwined. She is one of the many accomplished women who count Jean Yancy, the Denver woman with a "mentoring bench" in her honor, as a mentor/friend. Though Jean had no specific experience in Barbara's business, which involves industrial construction, Jean had advised and encouraged many entrepreneurs, in areas from textiles and clothing to a company that specializes in mentoring as a business! Jean, for Barbara, has been "a wise, invaluable counsel." Over the years Jean has offered Barbara "honesty, integrity, candor, love, caring, and respect—those things," Barbara emphasized, "that make life work." Those are the qualities, also, that Barbara expected would form the basis of learning connections with her new "friends." "Women cannot separate friendship from mentoring," Barbara concluded. "I want women to learn from each other, but as friends."

Arlene Blum is another women whom many younger women would consider their mentor; yet Arlene, like Barbara, resists the label *mentor* in favor of the word *friend*. A former Berkeley chemistry professor, Arlene is best known as a mountaineer who led an all-female climbing expedition and wrote a book about her experience, *Annapurna: A Woman's Place*. Recently Arlene has been a leadership consultant and seminar presenter for major corporations.

Arlene claims that people have told her she had been their mentor, but she has never considered herself to be a mentor. Instead, she says, she has formed friendships with young female climbers and women she has met in her weekend retreats,"Climbing Your Own Everest."

"Very quickly," Arlene told me, "potential protégés become friends, and I learn as much from them about their lives and ambitions as they learn from me." Arlene does not feel that either she or the other woman is "better." Her friends have ideas and questions that challenge Arlene, and she shares with her friends what she has done and what she has learned.

Arlene's life is rich with friends all over the world. "If I were a mentor—and I prefer to be a friend," Arlene said as we ended our conversation, "I would describe my intentions in the words of a Buddhist prayer. I would like to increase the happiness and decrease the suffering of all sentient beings."

"Just being friends" does not mean that learning is not the acknowledged focus of the relationship. Often, as in the cases of Barbara and Arlene, the woman in the position to learn from the experienced women sees the relationship as one of mentoring, even if the "mentor" rejects that title. Susan Dundon, an opinion page columnist for the *Philadelphia Inquirer* and author of a novel, *To My Ex Husband,* considers the nationally syndicated columnist Ellen Goodman to be her mentor. For Susan, a mentor is someone "who is critical without being destructive, without taking away hope. She gives you a shot in the arm to go further."

For Susan, Ellen Goodman was one of those people who gave her a shot in the arm. Susan met Ellen through a mutual friend just after Ellen had become syndicated. Susan immediately liked Ellen as a person, and then she started reading her columns. When Ellen asked to see some of Susan's columns, Susan sent her a collection. Ellen wrote back giving Susan advice. "Ellen helped me to go into the bathroom, cry, come out, and send the damn thing somewhere else."

When I asked Ellen how she felt about her role as a mentor for Susan and, I assumed, other authors as well, Ellen wrote back that *mentor* was too formal a word for how she saw these relationships. "I guess I see myself as Susan's friend," she said. "We talk.

49

When she's been struggling, in one direction or another, I've told her what I know.

"Mentoring," Ellen continued, "sounds awfully formal and official. I think of Susan and me as peers. At work, of course, I talk to younger women and listen and help them focus. But still, it's more informal than mentoring sounds to my ear."

These women who describe learning relationships as friendships are describing relationships in which women benefit from the caring, experience, and guidance of other women without the relationship being specifically labeled as one of "mentoring." The mentors, or more experienced women, identify themselves as friends or equals, providing what help they can to another women in her quest for learning and achievement.

In All but Name: The Unnamed Coach, Counselor, Advocate

Many younger women with whom I have met would not feel comfortable calling their learning connection with an older or more experienced woman a friendship. It would seem too intimate and presumptive. Neither do they want to use the word *mentor* for fear that it sounds too formal, too rigid, too heavy with expectation and obligation.

"I would never use the word *mentoring* with Monica," a twenty-four-year-old woman from a Chicago consulting firm told me during a focus group lunch. "If she knew that I see her as a mentor, maybe the relationship would go away. It's better that we never acknowledge a mentor/protégé connection. I would be too uncomfortable if we did."

Andrea Auyer, the young woman who made this statement, was not the only woman at the lunch who could identify a woman as her mentor but was adamant about not using the word. "What if I referred to her as my mentor and she hadn't ever considered that we had a mentoring relationship?" Micky said. "I would feel I'd been rude and overstepped my boundaries. I would be so embarrassed!"

Woman like Andrea feel that the idea of burdening someone we respect and admire with our own needs is intrusive. These women are polite, considerate, and concerned about exploiting a connection. They don't want to push, but they do want to reach out to another woman as a resource from whom they can learn and develop. Andrea's preference is to continue stopping by Monica's office when she has a question about her interactions with a client or about the firm's operation, questions she wouldn't ask her boss for fear of exposing an insecurity or lack of competence. However, Monica has volunteered suggestions, advice, and praise for Andrea, and Andrea values a "trust and special dimension" in their connection.

Sally Helgesen, author of *The Female Advantage*, is very clear about her understanding of why some women are reluctant to name the mentoring relationship. "When women are afraid to name the mentoring relationship," she explained to me over lunch in New York on a bright September day, "it's because they fear that the relationship won't be perceived as mutual, but rather as exploitative in some way."

For these women in no-name relationships, there can still be benefits. As long as the unannounced protégé believes that she is learning from her mentor, she has an advantage in her career. Even without the name *mentor*, junior women feel comfortable engaging in exploratory conversations with senior women about their development needs and career goals. They trust the senior women they approach to share their knowledge and experience, but they don't want to burden them with the title *mentor*. "I wouldn't want to burden a relationship by naming it mentoring," Andrea added. "Labeling puts on too much pressure for both people involved; the obligations become binding."

Some other women fear that labeling a connection "mentoring" might limit the warmth and growth potential within the relationship. A twenty-six year old woman who has worked as an advertising account executive in Chicago explained, "There is always the possibility that this woman I feel is my mentor could become my friend. The friendship feeling could go cold as soon as the mentoring concept comes in."

The unnamed learning relationship can work, as long as it doesn't hold you back from learning in deference to friendliness and dead-evenness.

Experience does have a lot to teach—you can take the lead, name or no name.

Though coaching and advocacy from influential people have been an important part of her professional growth, Cari Dominguez, a former partner at Heidrick & Struggles, an international executive search firm, and formerly assistant secretary for employment standards administration of the U.S. Department of Labor, has not openly referred to her sponsors as her mentors. For Cari, a mentor is someone who can coach, guide, and even intercede for you. A mentor can protect you from being fired or from getting into the line of "fire"; and is one who can find other places and opportunities for you. A mentor is a person who lets you know about things you'd never have known otherwise. She acknowledges having had "lots" of these relationships, mostly with men, but "the relationships have never been formally named or acknowledged. They just happened!"

And they happen, according to Cari, when the chemistry is right. They define themselves. They do not need to be acknowledged with a name. Cari does not advocate highly structured, regimented mentoring programs, which she considers artificial. She does, though, encourage women to become more savvy about finding potential supporters on their own who can share information and open doors.

"The best mentoring of all is informal," pronounced Sue Phillips, personnel manager for Openview Software, a division of Hewlett-Packard. "It is definitely mentoring, though it may feel like a friendship. It begins with affinity between two people, but the focus remains around work. It's a magical thing that happens when one person sees something in another person and wants to help that person grow." When it happens, Sue would say, don't let any hesitations hold you back.

The Informal Named Mentoring Connection

When the spontaneous connections happen, women frequently choose to recognize the relationship by giving it a name: mentoring. Madeleine Condit chooses to identify her learning partners, both men and women, as mentors. Madeleine is a partner with Korn/ Ferry International. Madeleine cultivated her mentoring relationships herself, without the formal intervention of a corporate program. Most of her mentors have been men, and she has had many mentors throughout her career.

I consider Madeleine's mentoring relationships to have been informal because they were not assigned or sanctioned by a formal mentoring program. Yet, the relationships still were based on a certain formality that is different from friendship or no-name relationships. "The formality of mentoring," Madeleine explained, "is approaching another person and saying, 'I need your help.'" She added, "Mentoring is a very sophisticated thing. You have to know yourself and your needs, and this takes savvy." In the case of Kaia and Darcy, Kaia said, "I need your help," and Darcy agreed. Though they are reluctant to burden the connection with the term *mentoring*, the purpose of their connection is clear. Theirs is an informal named mentoring relationship.

Though the nursing profession has a system of preceptors who are assigned to new nurses to help them develop their skills, opportunity still exists for protégés to find mentors within the formal structure. In the case of Diana Ward-Collins, currently an educator, MSN, medical legal consultant, and mediator, the informal mentoring relationship she established with Pat Fogelstrom at a California Hospital in 1963 continues to this day. When Diana came to work, Pat was director of a variety of clinical areas, including cancer research. Pat was a "calming" force who brought process awareness to Diana's emotional responses to issues. The relationship was "reciprocal," Diana remembers, with both women promoting each other through public praise and support.

Another example of informal mentoring comes from a telephone company. Karen, one of the company's few women vice presidents, talked with me about the people, mostly men, who have been her mentors. In Karen's career, more men than women have been available as mentors. You may have a similar situation in your career. Men are fine mentors for many women, and many women, like Karen, have appreciated the coaching, support, and entrée men have offered. When women have male mentors, chances are that the connection has a name. In Karen's case, the relationship she had with James, an executive some levels above her, was named—but informal. One day he called her into his office and said directly, "Let me coach you."

"Even though our relationship had no formal name," she said, "he was clearly my mentor. I knew it, and so did others in the company." The relationship had no written guidelines or goals, but the expectation was that James would advise and be a sounding board for Karen, and Karen would reciprocate with support and her own coaching for James, based on her observations and her skill with people management and communications.

Two other women discussed with me their experiences as protégés and mentors. Jeanne Canteen, vice president and general manager, is now retired. Her protégés, however, are still around and doing well. Jeanne has no problem with the word *mentor*, and she served as a mentor in informal relationships with a number of younger women. One of her protégés, Kitty Linder, is now Vice President of Operator Service/Operations. "When I first knew Kitty," Jeanne told me, "I was her boss and her coach. When I was no longer her boss, I became her mentor. In this situation, she could discuss her strengths with me more openly, and also her weaknesses."

Kitty's and Jeanne's was an informal, acknowledged mentoring relationship that has now become a friendship as well. But during the mentoring phase, both women knew the relationship and the obligations. "I would never mentor a woman without potential," Jeanne added. "And I never use the word *mentee*! I hate that word. I would rather use *friend*."

Assigned Mentors in Formal Mentoring Programs

"When I hear that a company has a formal mentoring program, I immediately know that they are referring to a program for women and minorities," an executive of a high-tech company told me when we sat together on a flight to New York. His company has such a program, and he believes that the process has achieved good results for the people involved.

Formal mentoring programs within organizations and professions give high-potential people, usually women and members of minority groups, access to upper-level managers and executives who can aid and advance their careers. Most often a selection process exists in which bosses or managers nominate a candidate to participate in the program. After a screening procedure, the prospective protégé is linked with a mentor, usually someone who has volunteered for the responsibility. Next follows training sessions for the participants in how to be protégés and mentors. The protégés meet with their mentors to identify goals, develop a contract, and schedule times to get together. Often the protégés are involved, as a group, in ongoing management or career seminars where their coming together and learning from one another adds value to the formal experience. Many of these programs have specific life spans and end with a celebration for protégés and their mentors.

It is not uncommon for people who have been part of a formal mentoring program, especially women, to tell me that they find these formal programs artificial and almost antithetical to the true meaning of mentoring, where "chemistry," "magic," and "affinity" inspire the learning relationship. However, many women and members of minority groups who would not have approached a potential mentor on their own can feel comfortable in a formal program and benefit enormously from the opportunity it gives. These programs are, after all, designed to expose junior people to the organization, to significant people within the organization, and to mentors with skills and abilities that have earned them recognition within the corporation. Formal programs, therefore, offer women access to coaches and counselors, along with opportunities for visibility and access to experiences they might not have had if they had had to produce or wait for an ideal mentoring match on their own. And sometimes within the formal relationship, participants discover an affinity that sparks a more spontaneous, informal, and long-lasting connection that might not have happened without the more formal introductions.

Often large corporations have accelerated development programs that target primarily high-potential women for an extremely structured relationship with a mentor that provides career planning, goal setting, evaluations, and excellent opportunities for visibility throughout the company. Mariah, president of her own consulting group and formerly with a Fortune 500 corporation, likes the program at her former employer because it is formal and written down. "It describes a two-way relationship with a framework and agreement and a no-fault termination," she explained. "When it's written down, it's depersonalized, and that works well for many people."

Cindy Furst was a member of the 1993 class of the Accelerated Development Program at Hewlett Packard Company, which had a total of twenty-four women. She is an advocate for what determined, talented women can learn through the goal setting, coaching, and exposure they receive in Hewlett-Packard's corporatewide program. "It is a formal situation," she said, "but one that is invaluable in terms of professional growth and opportunity. The intent is clear, and the work expected of both the protégé and the mentor is well spelled out."

Juanita Cox Burton, a retired executive director from US West in Englewood, Colorado, and a management consultant, believes emphatically that for minority women specifically, and for all women in general, formal programs offer opportunities that these women would never experience without the structure and security that formality lends. Juanita has benefited from informal mentoring in her career and has initiated formal programs for women and people of color.

One of Juanita's informal mentors was a white male in the 1970s. When he asked Juanita why he should hire her, she answered, "Because I am good." At the time, the 1970s, he didn't know what to do with a black woman, so Juanita suggested, "Let me help you know what it's like to be a black woman." She mentored him about black women, and he mentored her by giving her direction and opportunities. "He talked me up," she laughs. Some of Juanita's best mentoring came from a white female boss who took a risk of being called racist when she criticized Juanita's performance.

Because Juanita recognized the powerful benefit of having a mentor, she took the initiative to develop and direct a mentoring program at US West in the 1980s, the first such program to exist in corporate America. First she developed a support base for black women, white women, American Indian women, and Hispanic women who had previously had no one with whom to talk. At that time, one in 21 white men were being promoted, but only one in 138 white women and one in 386 women of color. Juanita's support base, a coalition of white women and people of color, went to management and asked for the Accelerated Development Program for women of color. Management gave her the go-ahead, and with her group she developed criteria for the protégés, including leadership experience, top performance, and a letter of recommendation from their bosses. They received 485 résumés for the first fifty slots. Every one of the protégés who received coaching and counseling through the program got promoted at least once. It is Juanita's absolute conviction that only one or two of the women in the first program would ever have pursued a mentoring relationship if they hadn't had a formal program to back them. Through the program, these women became visible to upper managers. They attended dinners at which all officers and directors were present. It gave them a chance to build allies and make contacts that they would never have had otherwise. "Even women not in the program," Juanita noted, "benefited from the visibility these high-performance women gained." The program won the coveted Catalyst Award in 1989.

At the John Hancock Mutual Life Insurance Company in Boston, a formal mentor/protégé program is in its early stages. The pilot program has twenty-one pairs, determined after a rigorous selection procedure. Karen Morton, second vice president and counsel, and Sandra Colley, director of workforce diversity, the people responsible for the program design, sees the mentoring project as a "way of facilitating growth of relationships that would not have happened spontaneously." As is often the case, the program has two objectives: (1) the development of individuals and (2) the development of diversity within the company. Pairs are cross-matched for race and gender, giving the mentors opportunities to learn from new populations while honing their own management and counseling skills. "What we have here," Janet realized, "is a corporately condoned context in which mentors can offer their pearls of wisdom."

The Catalyst organization in New York has put together an excellent publication on how to set up a mentoring program within a corporation—a fine resource if your company is considering such a project.

Cross-Organizational Formal Mentoring Opportunities

For women who don't work for corporations that offer formal mentoring programs, outside programs designed to enhance skill base and career opportunities do exist. Once such program is Women Unlimited, a twelve-month program designed to assist women in the achievement of more effective leadership and workplace diversity management skills. Jean Otte, founder and president of Women Unlimited, Inc., a nonprofit organization, was corporate vice president of quality management for National Rental Car System, Inc. She has received certification as an examiner for the Malcolm Baldrige

National Quality Award. The protégés in her Women Unlimited program are women with usually one to five years of management experience who have the potential to become mid- to senior-level management candidates. Mentors for the program are men and women who currently hold, or have held, mid- to senior-level management positions for a minimum of five years. Women, often selected by their corporations, apply for the program, and they or their corporations pay more than $2,000 for the year. The intention of the program is to pair these women with mentors in industries other than their own from whom they can gain new perspectives and broaden their diversity knowledge and leadership skills. I attended one of the many workshops scheduled in addition to meetings with mentors throughout the year.

The women participants felt they were gaining extremely valuable knowledge and experience through the formal program, not only from their mentors but also from getting to know the other highly motivated and capable women protégés.

Formal mentoring programs exist in government agencies, universities, professional organizations, and corporations. The Small Business Administration has an excellent program for women in business that pairs entrepreneurs and protégés with women who have volunteered their time and expertise.

Becoming part of a formal mentoring program does not mean you cannot also learn from friends, bosses, no-name relationships, or informal connections. What is important is that you reach out to other people who have the knowledge and the resources to support your goals and get you where you want to go.

The Right Connection for You

What is the right connection for you? The right connection is the one in which you feel comfortable, in which you have the right woman as your learning partner, and in which you are committed to take advantage of the resource available to you. You may have a mentor who sees you as a friend at the same time as you have a named mentoring connection with another woman in your profession at the same time as you have a female mentor through a formal program in your company. What is important is that you recognize and seize the opportunity to connect with other women in learning partnerships. The following chapters will guide you in selecting the right woman at the right time and in preparing to make the most of what she has to offer. Women are waiting to mentor you, to instruct and guide you, and to celebrate as you both live well with your achievements.

If You Want to Learn More

Belenky, Mary Field, Blythe McVicker Clinchy, Nancy Rule Goldberger, and Jill Mattuck Tarule. *Women's Ways of Knowing: The Development of Self, Voice, and Mind* (New York: Basic Books, 1986).

Gilligan, Carol. *In a Different Voice* (Cambridge, Mass.: Harvard University Press, 1982).

Schaef, Anne Wilson. *Women's Reality* (Akron, Oh.: Winston Press, 1981).

CHAPTER 5

Preparing to Be a Protégé

LANIE'S STORY

Lanie folded her raincoat into the overhead bin, worked her briefcase and purse under the seat in front of her, and settled into her seat for the four-hour flight to San Francisco. Just six months ago Lanie had moved into a marketing position in the Colorado division of a high-tech computer products company. Once in the air, she adjusted her seat backward and closed her eyes for a few minutes of quiet and thoughtfulness. From the time she had arrived at her new desk, the intense pace had kept her in constant action. Lanie loved the challenge and significance of her new job. Her boss had told her that she was doing well, and she already saw opportunities to advance within the company.

Lanie knew that she had the skills and focus to fit in and to succeed in this fast-paced, productivity-focused culture, but everything was happening so fast! She hadn't had time to consider her future beyond preparing for the immediate challenge of the next project. She thrived on her job and wanted a career, but she also wanted a whole life beyond the landscaped campus of her division headquarters. Lanie felt as if she were levitating a few feet above what she was doing, watching herself, always conscious of how she should be performing and behaving—and never quite comfortable that she was "okay." She didn't really feel like herself, and she needed to talk to someone who could understand. She needed a place where she could feel grounded, be herself, and be known and appreciated as herself.

To bring her career and life back into sync, Lanie needed a woman to talk with—a woman who would listen and empathize. She needed to connect with an ambitious, successful woman who knew firsthand how a female could achieve and survive as herself in this corporation's male-dominated culture. She also needed someone who could see the big picture, a woman with position and power who was willing to extend her knowledge and influence to a talented junior hoping to follow in her wake.

As the plane hummed westward, Lanie realized that she had been thinking about having a woman mentor. Not because she wouldn't appreciate and benefit from having a man mentor with knowledge to share and influence to pave the way. In fact, Paul, two levels above her, had noticed her abilities and had gone out of his way to publicly complement her performance. He could be a valuable connection. To have him as a mentor would be a great opportunity, one that she would accept with appreciation.

Paul, she knew, could show her the ropes, even pull some important strings if she continued to perform up to his expectations. But would he have the knowledge, the wisdom of a woman's experience, to guide Lanie through the choices that affect a woman's future and her satisfaction with her career and life balance? Though well intended and certainly sincere, would he be mentoring Lanie to become one with the male culture of their organization? Could she be her authentic self with Paul without having to translate for him the essence of her female self, which she honored and was determined to retain? Would she protect her career advantage of having Paul as a mentor by concealing emotional or personal priority issues that he might consider insignificant or even detrimental to her career direction? Though Paul would be a valuable ally, Lanie knew that she needed to find a woman who could get to the core of Lanie's challenges and quests.

Lanie remembered how her sister Suzan, a nurse, had found such a woman to be her sounding board and guide. Darlene, whom Suzan had met when the senior woman presented a seminar at Suzan's hospital, had raised a family while continuing to work full time and add degrees to her credentials. Suzan had been at an impasse in her own career development. She needed to work, to contribute her share to the family income. The next step in her career would be a master's degree with a clinical specialty, but did she have the time or really the desire to do that at this point in her life? Would she be compromising her time with her two children and her husband if she put those few free hours she had into classes and study? And what would it gain for her? Darlene had listened and understood. She had respected Suzan's career goals and her family priorities. She'd been there, and she could see over the hills Suzan saw as mountains. Together, Darlene and Suzan designed a plan where Suzan would take special training in home infusion therapy and develop an expertise that would add to her options without denying her the time with her family. Suzan had been honest with Darlene about her career goals, her needs as a mother and wife, and her confusion about the impact of her decisions on her life and on her career. Darlene had been a wonderful mentor for Suzan, and Lanie hoped that she too could find a woman with whom she could be her honest, genuine self and benefit from the experience, wisdom, and knowledge that would help her achieve satisfaction in her career and her life.

Not One, but Many!

At this moment, Lanie was thinking in terms of the one, or maybe the one male and one female, mentor who can scan the skies and prepare her for future flight. In fact, though, Lanie, and you, throughout your life and career, will most likely have multiple mentors.

Janet Dreyfus Gray, Ph.D., is a consultant based in Mamaroneck, New York, who has designed and implemented numerous successful mentoring programs. Gray believes emphatically that:

> If there is anything that can influence a career more than a mentor, it's many mentors. This concept of nurturing role models in all facets of life fits a fast-changing world where it is necessary to adapt to ever-changing technology, intense competition, downsizing, mergers, and reorganizations. Because turnover is rapid everywhere, even if we were able to identify a "perfect mentor," there is no guarantee that she would be with the same organization or location in a year.

In their book *Mentors: The Most Obvious yet Overlooked Key to Achieving More in Life Than You Ever Dreamed Possible: A Success Guide for Mentors and Proteges*, Floyd Wickman and Terri L.

Sjodin referred to primary and secondary mentors. Your primary mentor would be a person whose experience, professional level, and commitment to you cover all, or most, areas related to your career and life development. Typically, she would be two or more levels above you in a corporate system, be well versed in the ways of the workplace, and have the styles and skills necessary for success. Your secondary mentor would be someone who specializes in one area, perhaps negotiation skills, budget management, or opening international markets. Most likely you will spend more time with your primary mentor than with your secondary mentors. You will have scheduled meetings with your primary mentor at regular intervals, but you may call your secondary mentors only when you need information or guidance in a specific area.

Your primary mentor may transfer to another functional area or move to another corporation. Of course, she is continuing to build her career and is not obligated to limit her horizons in order to be there for you until retirement. In some cases she will remain your mentor and the two of you will gain advantage from increased exposure and experience within the corporation or industry. You will seek other mentors for the short term to guide you through a challenging life/career transition or through a specific project. I have mentored women who have wanted to write and publish a book. I give what I can, and when the project is complete, we no longer schedule regular meetings or phone calls. Though in most cases we keep in touch, essentially our mentoring connection has run its course.

Of course, there may also be a woman in an area not directly related to your career who wants to encourage your talents and potential and will be there as your supporter and advocate for life. She will be your superior mentor, the woman to whom you return for a reality check, a confidence boost, encouragement, or to recharge your vision and personal goals.

Also, appreciate that a "friend" can become a mentor when you ask for or she offers coaching or counseling from the perspective of her work or life experience. You may have casual, informal mentors within your profession whom you see or talk with only two or three times a year, but from whom you learn something each time and come away enriched. You may be assigned a mentor within a formal program and meet with her or him on a regularly scheduled basis with specific goals, objectives, assignments, and update reports. All these people have the potential to contribute to your career achievement and to your life. They have gifts to offer. You would be well advised to seek these gifts and respond by being prepared to learn, respectful of the opportunity, and appreciative of what you gain. Your mentors become your network. With your women mentors you will form a network of women vested in one another's success through the act of giving. It then becomes your turn, your opportunity to expand this network by becoming a mentor for women who are following in your path.

Becoming a Responsible Protégé

Before Lanie decides to initiate a mentoring connection with an upper-level woman at work or to accept the opportunity to be mentored by a woman who recognizes her potential, she should learn what being a good protégé entails. She should consider how her role as a responsible protégé can enhance the mentoring experience for herself and for her mentor. As well as being prepared to benefit professionally, she will be able to anticipate and avoid common pitfalls and contribute to the value of the mentoring connection for herself and for her mentor.

How to Prepare

Before you consider entering a mentoring relationship, prepare yourself to be a good protégé. "Instead of fretting about who will make a good mentor," Dr. Linda Hill of the Harvard Business School tells us in her article "Managing Your Career":

> successful managers focus on being a 'good protégé' so others will be attracted to working with them. They rec-

ognize that mentoring relationships demand considerable investment and risk on the part of both partners. They share responsibility with their mentors for ensuring that the relationship is productive and mutually beneficial; they make an effort to give back as much as they receive.

Mentoring, especially when women mentor women, involves risk for both the protégé and the mentor. A high-profile woman mentoring a female rising star, for example, attracts attention. Larin Lenke in *Women and Leadership* cited researchers Ragins and Cotton when she wrote. "Given the limelight focused on the token woman, the failure of a protégé is a much greater risk for a woman executive than it is for a man. . . . Mistakes made by women mentors in guiding the careers and advancement of other women are often evaluated more harshly." The protégé who respects this risk will make every effort to support the success of the relationship— for herself and for her mentor.

As a protégé you will be responsible for excellent performance on work related opportunities as well as for sensitive and respectful management of the mentoring relationship.

Are You Ready?

To assess your readiness to be a protégé of a female mentor and benefit from the woman-to-woman connection, ask yourself the following questions and answer honestly. To the extent that you are not sure or not willing, you are not yet ready to be a committed protégé. With more workplace experience and appreciation of what mentoring can give, you may change your mind and become an attractive and receptive protégé.

Read the question and choose the number that represents your spontaneous response:

	Yes, I definitely am.	I'm not sure.	No, I couldn't do that.
1. I am comfortable with the idea of forming a constructive learning and developmental relationship with a woman who has the power and influence to advance my career and affect the direction of my life.	❐	❐	❐
2. I am willing to enter into a respectful relationship with a woman who, based on her experience and position in the hierarchy, is considered "superior" to me.	❐	❐	❐
3. I am ready to accept constructive, critical feedback from a woman.	❐	❐	❐
4. I am willing to publicly support my female mentor.	❐	❐	❐
5. I am prepared to enter a reciprocal relationship in which I will provide my mentor with information and feedback that can help her advance in her career and enhance her life.	❐	❐	❐

	Yes, I definitely am.	I'm not sure.	No, I couldn't do that.
6. I am prepared for my mentor to at times be too busy to advise or consult with me.	☐	☐	☐

Take seriously those questions you answered "I'm not sure." or "No, I couldn't do that." Negative responses represent potential challenges to the protégé/mentor relationship. Try to understand why you answered the way you did and how you might learn to change your response or to work with your attitudes in a positive and nondestructive manner.

Learning From an Accomplished Woman

If, even having read this far into this book, you are still not sure that you are ready to identify yourself with a female mentor who could have considerable power over the direction of your career and your life, wait before committing yourself to a named mentoring relationship. The expectations for a trusting, supportive connection may feel too constrictive, and you could unconsciously sabotage the success of the connection and ruin both your and your mentor's opportunities for successful mentoring connections in the future. You may be more at ease and authentic in an informal, unnamed connection where you can ask for specific guidance when you need insight or direction without the ongoing obligation of a committed mentoring relationship. Becoming part of a relationship in which you hesitate or hold back can predestine you to disappointment with the connection. Your ambivalence will carry the seed of destruction. Don't become a protégé because others believe in the value and power of the opportunity. You will know when you are ready.

You can still succeed and achieve if you choose not to pursue a mentor or respond to an invitation from a prospective mentor. You can form connections in other ways and learn by observing rather than by establishing a personal basis for information sharing and guidance. Dr. Judy Rosener, author of *America's Competitive Secret Women Managers* and a strong advocate for women and the contributions they make to management and leadership in the American workplace, told me that she finds the emphasis on mentoring to be overdone. She says that while mentors can be helpful, the best way for women to advance is to look around, learn from everyone with whom they work, develop their strengths, and build on what they learn. In other words, there are mentors all around, we just don't call them that. So, perhaps you will find yourself acting as a mentor before you have been a protégé. To Rosener, mentoring is helping, and you are surrounded by people who can help.

Appreciating Hierarchy

Some women are uncomfortable with hierarchy, or nonpeerness, in their woman-to-woman relationships. These women feel most comfortable with women they perceive to be "like" themselves in status, be it career stage, salary level, or professional position. After all, haven't we been told that women include others and willingly share information and power? She's not supposed to be superior to me, some women conclude, and she'd better not flaunt her position when I'm around!

Kris, a female associate in a West Coast architectural firm with offices in three cities, told me that she had no problem meeting male principals from her firm at the airport and taking them to dinner. However, when she was to meet a female principal, her superior on the career ladder, and escort her to dinner, she felt insecure, confused, and defensive. Frequently the dinner proceeded in tense silence, with little information or friendliness exchanged.

Relating to another woman in a hierarchical context was disorienting for Kris. She discovered how entrenched in her was the myth that women's relationships must be built on our sameness and that difference, especially in a one-up sense, is inherently competitive and "unnatural." Kris acknowledged that she would have to work on understanding her reactions before she would feel comfortable enough with a woman of superior position to benefit from having her as a mentor. Women who have gone before us in our professions and corporations have achieved for themselves and, by association, for all women. Many of these women are waiting and willing to reach back and bring another woman along.

Instead of fighting for what Dr. Pat Heim refers to in her seminars as the "dead even rule," those of us who can look up with appreciation will benefit most if we respect the talents and accomplishments of our high-achieving sisters and prepare ourselves to learn from their success. Those who lead will welcome and honor our acknowledgment, and we will move ahead more quickly and satisfactorily with our careers and our lives. In the end, the female workplace network will benefit from our mutual support and strength.

Getting Ready for the Critique

One of the career-enhancing advantages that is often denied women is access to constructive, critical feedback. Men have been reluctant to criticize women for fear of appearing sexist and implying that women aren't as good at work as men. Women, whose gender-culture traditions emphasize kindness and togetherness, have also been reluctant to provide other women with vital, critical feedback. To compound the challenge, women have a reputation for "taking it personally" and interpreting criticism of their performance as a rejection of themselves as people. As women, we are extremely sensitive to the possibility that another woman will overpersonalize our well-intended feedback and be hurt by our criticism. Reactions to being hurt can range from withdrawing from the woman who criticizes to punishing her with destructive back stabbing and public attacks on her performance and credibility. As a result, many women are unwilling to be honest and fair in their constructive criticisms of other women.

Protégés, however, must be willing and able to hear and accept critical feedback from their female mentors. Constructive, honest criticism and positive encouragement are vital elements in a powerful mentoring relationship. Juanita Cox Burton, an African American woman formerly with US West and currently a sought-after workplace consultant, said she benefited enormously from a white woman who mentored her by helping her develop "tact" and correct her grammar. Like many of the women I have interviewed, Juanita mentioned critical feedback as one of the most beneficial aspects of a woman-to-woman mentoring relationship. We need to hear from a woman's perspective how our performance measures up, and we can benefit from this learning only if we are receptive to criticism and refuse to interpret "You can improve" as "I'm not good enough" or "You don't like me."

You can encourage your mentor to provide you with vital criticism by confronting the issue directly. Tell her that you realize she may be reluctant to be honest and harsh with you, and that you value her perspective and want to hear everything she has to offer. With this permission, follow through and accept her critique as a gift. Take careful note of her suggestions and let her know the results you are achieving.

Can You Do Your Part?

I cannot emphasize enough that a successful protégé is one who understands her reciprocal role in the mentoring relationship. Your woman mentor is holding the golden grail ready to pour gallons of how-to punch into your big gulp cup. Though your mentor is your leader and teacher, your wise adviser and opener of doors, she is in a position to learn from you as well. The woman-to-woman mentoring relationship is grounded in mutuality and partnership. Your mentor will direct you to projects and people that will strengthen your experience and develop your skills base. You will keep her informed of training you have attended and changes in the customer base, and even provide her with feedback or coaching points on how she presented the new initiative to the board at your company's annual meeting. As she shares her stories with you, you will listen attentively and encourage her to synthesize her experience and gain insights into her own effectiveness and style. You, as a listener and learner, can contribute to the mentoring experience by helping your mentor see and know herself as she shares with you the secrets of the system and the lessons she has learned.

Mentoring, for women, is a respectful gift exchange that acknowledges that two whole persons are involved in a learning and growth-focused process. Elizabeth, now a vice president at a large eastern communications company, was called into her mentor's office one Christmas Eve a few years ago. What her mentor, Donna, wanted to know was how Donna could improve her people skills. She was an excellent manager of facts and figures, a financial wizard, but she wanted to become a better communicator and listener. She asked Elizabeth to help her, and Elizabeth was able to give her some valuable feedback and suggestions, which Donna appreciated, put into practice, and thanked Elizabeth for privately and publicly.

You may be unsure about the proper protocol for offering information and feedback to a senior women. Don't be; she needs your feedback. If your mentor does not directly ask you for information to help her, but you know something that would give her advantage or enhance her knowledge base, it is your responsibility within the relationship to share the information with her. As a mentor, she is giving you valuable time and energy, and one way you can reciprocate is by contributing to her strengths by offering what you know or have learned.

You must believe in your own potential if you are going to ask another woman to believe in you.

You cannot expect your mentor to invest in you if you do not consider yourself worth her effort! You want a mentor because you value yourself and your abilities and want to enhance your competence through the exchanges and insights of mentoring. It is important that you increase a mentor's confidence in you by demonstrating your commitment to the process—for both of you.

Supporting Her in Public

One element of the reciprocal relationship between protégé and mentor is that the protégé publicly supports the woman who is mentoring her. This public support can mean defending the mentor's contributions at staff meetings, developing a base of receptivity for her ideas among peers, or referring to her achievements at corporate gatherings and in networking situations. Most women who want to be protégés welcome the opportunity to promote and advocate for other women. If, however, you feel uncertain about openly promoting and being identified with "weak" women as opposed to "strong" men, you are not in a position to learn from a female mentor. Also, if you hesitate to be seen as a "woman supporter" for fear you will be viewed by men as a threatening feminist, don't misrepresent yourself to a female mentor. She will recognize your reluctance to associate with her in public and, appropriately, feel her time and commitment to you have been misused. When you appreciate what your female mentor has accomplished and are enthusiastic about advertising her to your corporation or within your profession, then you are ready to approach her as a protégé!

When She Is Simply Too Busy

"One reason I hesitate to become a mentor again," Leslie, an editor in her early forties at a New York City publishing house, told me, "is that I couldn't deal with my last protégé's expectation that I was supposed to drop everything when she needed feedback or direction. It was as if since I was her mentor, I had more of an obligation

73

to her career than to maintaining and continuing to advance my own!"

Unfortunately, Leslie's experience with a demanding protégé has taken a marvelous mentor out of the pool, at least until she recovers from her disappointing experience. As a protégé, you select a woman to mentor you because she is successful and has the values, skills, and traits you admire. Remember, though, that she still has her own life and her own career to manage. Understand that mentoring you is not her only and most likely not even her first priority. Honor her schedule and her stresses, and don't expect to be able to barge in on her at any time. It is best if you can plan ahead to meet at a time convenient for both of you—a time she agrees to when she will be prepared to give you her full attention. She will recognize your respectful consideration, and the time you spend together will be more satisfying for both of you.

What About Your Boss and Your Coworkers?

The woman you approach to be your mentor, or the person who identifies you as her protégé, will not be your current boss. Though your boss can be instrumental in your performance development and career growth, your interactions with a boss who directs and evaluates you are different from your relationship with your mentor. Your boss is responsible for keeping her projects and department or group performance looking good. You as an employee play a role in how well she delivers on the bottom line. She develops you to contribute to her work plan and values you as you make her and her department look good. Your boss does not have the commitment to developing the full range of your potential as does your mentor. She may not want you to advance beyond her area; rather, she may want to keep you because you are a good performer, or because diversity initiatives favor departments with a good representation of women and people of color.

You will want to look good to your boss and develop her confidence in you as a first rate contributor. Whereas you will share failures with your mentor so that you can understand what went wrong and prepare to succeed next time, you will want to emphasize your successes with a boss who is responsible for your evaluations and salary.

You and your boss will work on development plans for your future, and here is an opportunity for you to include your mentor. Let your boss know that you have a mentor and how you see your mentor affecting your development and your future. Your boss may at first resist or resent the intrusion of a mentor into her area of responsibility for your development. It is up to you to assure your boss that you want to be open about the mentoring connection. It is not uncommon for a mentor to sit in with her protégé and her protégé's boss when they review performance and create a development plan for the year. It may be, for example, that your mentor can include you in project activities that will be good for your experience and developing skills and will also benefit your boss's long-term plans for expanding her department.

If your mentor is at a higher level than your boss and holds a position of power over your boss's area, it is understandable that your boss may be resentful and even jealous of your opportunity. You can turn the situation to mutual advantage if, with your mentor's agreement, you share information about the organization with your boss and keep your boss current on organizational issues. Your mentor than becomes a resource for your boss as well, and all of you benefit from shared information and constructive, company-focused goals.

Your peers, too, may not respond with cries of joy and celebration when they learn that you have been selected for a fast-track mentoring program or have acknowledged an informal mentoring connection with a person of greater position and influence. Women I have spoken with in an international corporation that has a formal fast-track program and in a smaller company that encourages successful women to reach back and mentor promising junior woman are clear in their resentment of the rising stars. Those who have been left out of the prime development game see aggressive protégés as women using other women to leverage their advancement needs, not as women wanting to gain life knowledge from an accomplished woman and develop as a whole and complete person. "These women on the fast track, the ones with mentors in high places, are not interested in women's causes," women at the international corporation tell me. "They don't look around them, they only look up. They are interested only in themselves and their future."

The women I interviewed who are on the fast track and have organizational coaches or personal mentors are aware of these feelings among some of their peers. Those with women coaches or mentors are committed to enhancing opportunities for all women in their corporation. They see their senior women mentors as being in a new role, perceived as different by both men and women, and under heavy scrutiny. They see their roles as protégés as part of the support system these pioneering women need if they are to maintain the place they have achieved in a male-oriented organization. They are committed to publicly supporting their mentors, now senior executives, at all levels within the corporation.

One way to defuse the resentment of your mentoring advantage that some of your peers may feel is to include them. Talk about how your mentoring arrangement works and share some of the information and tips you are getting from your mentor. One woman, Cynthia, whose colleague Angie was not chosen for a select mentoring program became herself a peer, or horizontal, mentor for her coworker. She regularly shared with Angie what she and her mentor were discussing. Through her mentor, Cynthia learned of an executive development program at Northwestern University and encouraged Angie to apply. Both women ended up attending and benefiting from the experience—which they have plans to share with others.

What Mentors Want You to Know

You have thought about your preparedness to present yourself as a protégé in a mentoring relationship. You are ready to pursue the opportunity to be mentored and to benefit from the experience. Before leaving this chapter, please consider seriously the following requests that experienced mentors would make of a prospective protégé. I have synthesized this list of six expectations from the many interviews I have had with mentors in high-level positions, with mentors who have advanced experience in their professions, with entrepreneurs, and with educators at the high school and university levels. Their advice is convincingly similar and universally applicable. Following their direction will make you an attractive protégé and contribute to a successful and mutually beneficial mentoring connection.

Have Specific Goals

Develop specific goals for your mentoring connection, and make these goals clear. Whether you are asking your friend for a mentoring moment or writing a contract with your formal, assigned mentor, knowing your goals for the learning opportunity will help assure a satisfying mentoring experience.

For some of us, the thought of approaching a friend with goals that you want her to help you accomplish seems calculated and coldly impersonal. However, when you have a specific goal in mind, you help your friend focus on your current situation and avoid spending valuable time wandering around the issue. It may be that you want to leave your present job and find another a notch up in your profession. Or perhaps your friend is feeling stonewalled by a colleague and is seeking your help in resolving the situation. When you know the goal, you can help keep your mentoring conversation on track and get the guidance you need. When you attain your goal, you and your friend will both understand the accomplishment and have reason to say thank you and celebrate.

Having goals also provides the substance for your informal and formal mentoring relationships. Goals help you guide the mentoring messages. For example, you can say to your mentor, "We have talked about my goal for moving from design into management. Tomorrow I have a meeting with Bert about the open management position. Can you help me make a great presentation?" Your mentor

77

knows what you want to accomplish, your goal, and she knows that you have met one of your objectives, to get an interview. She also knows that today you want to focus on your interview presentation. Your stated goals have prepared both of you for this mentoring session. The two of you can get right down to reviewing your résumé and materials with the goal in focus. Throughout the mentoring relationship, knowing and sharing your goals will help you achieve more constructive mentoring than if you arrive without focus, asking your mentor to "help you get ahead." Goals make the mentoring experience easier and more rewarding for both you and your mentor.

Goals are an important part of successful mentoring when you ask a friend to mentor you, when you approach a woman in an informal context and ask for her guidance, and, of course, when you work through a contract in a formal mentoring situation.

In formal or assigned mentoring, goals are part of the contract. I have seen notebooks full of material given to mentors and protégés in corporate assigned mentoring programs. Together, the protégé and her mentor determine career goals and prioritize those goals to determine what is the most effective focus for the time frame of the relationship, be it six months or a year. Once the goals are determined, the next step is to identify what must happen to achieve those goals. If the goal is to move into a project management position, you determine what training or experience you will need in order to be competitive. Next, you identify objectives that you must achieve in the path to your goal, such as taking certain training classes or volunteering to participate on high-profile projects. Your contract will most likely include a time chart with checkpoints to determine how you are proceeding in gaining the skills and experience you need in order to achieve your goal. You may develop a chart, or plan, that identifies what action your mentor expects you to take toward achieving your objectives and what action she agrees to take in support of your objectives and your goal. Your contract is a structured, objective agreement that allows you and your mentor to stay on track, use your time together well, and evaluate your progress.

A structured contract in a named mentoring relationship does not in any way preclude the holistic mentoring for which women can be such rich and wise resources. Often we use stories of our lives and our struggles to give context to a suggestion, be it whether to transfer to Boston or how to deal with the old school management group in Baltimore. Our career goals are not separate from our lives. Choices concerning how to accomplish those goals or even whether they are desirable and consistent with our life ambitions become part of the mentoring exchange. Our careers, like our lives, are growing, evolving experiences through which our mentors are our resources and our guides. Having goals, even if they change, gives us a point of reference, a starting—and even stopping—point that contributes structure to the mentoring relationship and supports the constructive connection.

When you talk with your mentor, have specific questions ready. When you have scheduled valuable time with your mentor, don't waste the moment by not being prepared. It doesn't help your mentor focus on your needs when you just say, "What do you think I should go after next?" Instead, offer some alternative possibilities you have identified for your next move and ask her what she thinks about the options. If a training workshop on designed experiments is being held in Chicago and another on project management is being offered at the same time in San Francisco, ask her which she thinks best fits with your talents, interests, and long-term goals. Be prepared to give her a copy of the training announcements and all information you have gathered about the selection process and funding for the training. The more she knows, the better she can help you explore your options and guide your decisions.

Help Your Mentor Focus Constructive Feedback

Don't just ask, "How am I doing?" Ask for specific information about how the presentation you gave went at the meeting your mentor attended, or how she thinks you handled the negotiations with the Detroit team. Let your mentor know your victories and frustrations. Ask if she has had similar struggles or if she has known others who have. Encourage her to tell you the stories and to extract the lessons that pertain to your situation and goals.

One of the characteristics of valuable woman to woman mentoring connections is that we can, and we should, share the stories of our failures as well as the tales of our triumphs.

If your mentor can be open with you about her mistakes and misfires, you can both gain insight and strength as she reviews her failure and analyzes the reasons why.

When she constructively criticizes herself and keeps the focus on the lessons she learned, she will encourage you to accept her constructive criticisms as opportunities to grow and try again.

Support Your Mentor With Positive Comments to Your Colleagues and to Her Bosses

A mentoring relationship is a reciprocal relationship, and supporting your mentor is one of your responsibilities. You are her protégé because you admire her accomplishments, values, and style. She is giving you the gifts of her experience and influence. Acknowledge those gifts by publicly supporting her value and her vision.

Put the Mentoring Into Action!

Let your mentor know what decisions you have made based on her information, and share with her the results of those decisions. Let her know how the new techniques worked at your Atlanta presentation. Keep her informed of your activities and accomplishments. She will think she is wasting her time if you don't indicate that you have implemented her thoughtful suggestions and guidance.

Also let her know when her suggestions don't work out or question why the meeting with Pat from San Jose came to a dead end. She needs the feedback from you to assess her strengths and strategies and to understand what is best for you and her as a mentoring pair. Her reputation is affected by your performance. She needs to know how her effectiveness as a mentor is perceived by her colleagues and superiors, and you are in an excellent position to bring her that information!

Finally, be sure to let her know when you have received a compliment in an area the two of you have worked on together! Passing on good news is equally as important as being honest about the mistakes and misfires.

Respond to Opportunities!

Let your mentor know the results of your meeting with Thomason and how you plan to follow up. Keep her informed on the new products project. Where time is tight, send her a note or an E-mail message. The point is to keep her informed, both out of courtesy and so that she can better assess your readiness for a new assignment. Knowing whom you met in Atlanta, for example, can give her the opportunity to open the next door and introduce you to the CFO who once worked with your Atlanta contact. She needs to know how her protégé is succeeding with her colleagues, and how to further support and direct your achievements.

Don't Expect a Promotion

Your mentor is not responsible for getting you a promotion, nor should she be. Her function is to coach and guide you in your career and life development so that you are prepared to benefit from opportunities when they present themselves. Your mentor enhances your worth, you get the job. She can discover for you where the opportunities are, she can help coach you in the skills you will need, and she can "talk you up" with her colleagues and connections. She can certainly help smooth the way, but she can't promise you the job.

When I talked with a group of women who are and have been mentors and protégés at NYNEX (now Bell Atlantic) in Syracuse, N.Y., they made the point again and again that mentoring was not about being promoted. Especially in a downsizing environment, promotions may simply not be available. However, mentoring retains its value as an opportunity for women to learn from their more experienced sisters. The NYNEX women valued their mentors for teaching them how to read the organizational winds and work toward making themselves "indispensable." It was their women mentors who were most sensitive to the whole life issues and who guided them in adjusting their goals to emphasize rewarding and balanced lives.

Say Thank You When You Say Good Bye

Don't just disappear when you have reached your goals or outgrown the mentoring connection. Thank your mentor for what you have learned and let her know why you are ending the structured phase of the relationship. She will appreciate knowing that she is no longer responsible for observing your performance or running your campaign. She will respect your professionalism and consideration and will most likely remain available to give you guidance and encouragement when you ask.

Developing the art of the protégé will continue as you go on to establish mentoring connections and move through your career and your life. Becoming a mentor yourself will further teach you how to succeed as a protégé. The gift extends and keeps giving.

You can start to mentor right now. Someone three months behind you in your career or your profession can benefit from what you are learning and from your counsel and support. You and your protégé can learn together to benefit from a woman-to-woman mentoring relationship.

If You Want to Learn More

Wickman, Floyd, and Terri L. Sjodin. *Mentoring* (Burr Ridge, Ill.: Irwin Professional Publishers, 1996).

Zey, Michael G. *The Mentor Connection: Strategic Alliances in Corporate Life* (New Brunswick, N.J.: Transaction Publishers, 1993).

CHAPTER 6

Identifying the Woman to Be Your Mentor

MARCIE'S STORY

Marcie, a training manager for a computer parts company, had been hesitant to approach Judith, the corporate training director, and ask if Judith would be her mentor. Instead of "coming right out and asking her directly," Marcie remembers, "I asked Judith if it would be all right if I told one of the managers that she had been my mentor." Marcie remembers being pleased when Judith responded that certainly Marcie could use her name, and that she would like to continue as Marcie's mentor if that was agreeable to Marcie. They agreed to meet after work the next Thursday to discuss each other's expectations for the mentoring experience, get to know each other better, and review their goals for Marcie's future.

Like Marcie, protégés who prefer that a mentoring relationship be named and mutually acknowledged face the dilemma of how to approach a potential mentor and ask to be mentored. If your organization has a formal coaching or mentoring program, investigate the process for becoming a protégé candidate. Marcie would have liked the formality and openness of such an arrangement, but her company had no official or formal mentoring program. If your organization has a mentoring program in place, learn all you can about who participates and how the program has been evaluated by past protégés and their mentors. Even if the program is open to anyone who is interested, you will most likely have to go through an application process. This process can include personal interest inventories, résumés, interviews with individuals or committees, and recommendations from your boss or manager before you are selected to be matched with a mentor.

In other instances, you must be invited—some call it "tapped"—to participate in a fast-track mentoring program for high-potential women. I have even had conversations with upper-level executives who acknowledge that their corporations have rising-star, push-them-ahead programs for high-potential women, but that the women in these programs do not know who their "secret" mentors are—or even that they have been identified for the fast-track program! The extra attention, training opportunities, and multiple challenges with high-level exposure should give a clue, but the fact is never stated.

Perhaps you are in a situation where no formal mentoring program exists, or perhaps you would rather make the mentoring connection on your own. Whatever the circumstances, approaching a woman and asking her to mentor you can be a daunting prospect.

Asking someone to take you under her wing and devote her time and energy to your career when she is still working on her own is making a huge request.

Approaching a woman to be your mentor within the organization means that you are asking her to identify with you, to take risks with your potential and with her own future. If you don't perform extremely well or if interpersonal conflicts damage your relationship in a public way, her judgment and management development skills may be brought into question. Essentially, you could both be dubbed failures.

Whether you are in the process of selecting a woman as your mentor or wondering if you should accept an invitation from a woman to be her protégé, the decision demands thoughtful and careful consideration. Having a woman mentor can be of enormous benefit to your career advancement and to your job and life satisfaction—if she is the right woman.

Who Should Be Your Mentor?

Whether a woman has approached you or you have decided to find a mentor on your own, you should ask yourself some basic questions before committing to the mentoring experience. Having the wrong woman as a mentor could cost both of you valuable time, energy, and confidence in the future.

I have compiled a list of questions to ask about a potential mentor based on the concerns women have shared with me from their experiences as protégés and as mentors. As you read through the questions a first time, permit yourself a spontaneous response. Trust your observations and your instincts. Then return to the questions and flesh out your reactions with lists of the potential mentor's skills and qualities, notes on what you have witnessed or heard about her from others, and any other behaviors or impressions that you have noted that could be relevant to her effectiveness as a mentor for you. By the time you have completed this exercise, you will have a strong basis on which to decide whether to pursue learning from this woman in a mentoring context. You will also have the background you need on your prospective mentor to support the conversation you plan for your initial meeting.

The questions in this exercise reflect what women tell me is important in establishing the right mentoring connection. Many women want more than a purely functional relationship with a high-powered person wearing a dress and blazer. They want and expect to connect with a multidimensional person in a learning relationship that considers and includes whole-life issues. You want to build a mentoring connection with a woman you can trust with the truth of yourself, and whom you can trust to offer you the truth of herself. When you can be your genuine, authentic self with another person, you can be most effectively open and receptive to what she can give and what she will teach.

To begin the exercise, as you read each question choose the answer that comes immediately to mind as you imagine a productive and compatible learning relationship with this other woman.

	Yes, definitely.	I'm not sure.	No, I don't think so.
1. Has this woman achieved a level of responsibility, influence, and recognition that represents what I want to achieve, if not ultimately, at least as a significant marker on my career journey?	❒	❒	❒
2. Is this woman in a position to guide me in attaining skills and developing abilities that complement my career goals?	❒	❒	❒
3. Is this a woman who has access to people and situations that can benefit my growth and career development?	❒	❒	❒
4. Am I comfortable with this woman's values?	❒	❒	❒
5. Would I be comfortable discussing my life-choice priorities with this woman?	❒	❒	❒
6. Do I genuinely like this woman?	❒	❒	❒

If you have spontaneously answered all questions "Yes, definitely," chances are that you have identified a woman with whom you could have a constructive and satisfying mentoring connection. However, a woman does not have to score a "1" in every category to be a positive mentor for you. You need to be conscious of what factors are most important for you and where you put the greatest emphasis. If, for example, you have evaluated a perspective mentor by answering "Yes, definitely" for questions 1, 2, and 3 but with a "I'm not sure" for 4, 5, and 6, she can still be an excellent career resource for you, if not your ideal named and acknowledged mentor. Having taken time to go through the worksheet, you will understand what you want from the mentoring connection and will be realistic about what this woman can and cannot provide.

Is She a Woman I Admire?

A little envy can be a good starting point for identifying someone you want to learn from at work. Envy means that you want what she has, and that can include position, power, salary, respect, and a seemingly smooth and balanced life. Ask yourself who has the level of responsibility and respect you would like to have. Note who has the reputation for excellent performance and the support of her colleagues, staff, or team that you want to achieve. Research who has the title and salary consistent with your ambition and goals. You may be surprised at the women you identify. They may not be in a straight line above you or even in your department or division. One may be a woman you know through a corporate or professional network who is moving ahead rapidly and managing her new positions with confidence, good performance, and a style you admire. Another may have been the chief financial officer for years, the only woman at the executive level, yet always approachable and universally respected by men and women.

Make a list of these women whom you envy and admire. For each, make notes on what it is that you admire about her and what she has achieved that you would like to achieve for yourself. Then continue your research by asking questions and reviewing her job history. Where did she begin? What is her educational and training background? Where else has she worked? Does she have a family, and how is she managing to balance her life and her career? Find out, if you can, if she has a mentor now and if she has had a mentor in the past. A woman who has benefited from a mentor appreciates the gifts she has received and is inclined to extend those gifts to others. Also, your mentor's mentor will be aware of you, and the connection can prove valuable. You will also want to learn if this woman has a current protégé and if that relationship is part of a formal development program or if it came about spontaneously. Of course, you will want to know how their relationship is perceived within the organization and how effective she has been in developing her current protégé. Perhaps you will learn that the relationship has worked well for both women and that the protégé is in the process of saying good-bye!

Learning as much as possible about a woman you admire and are considering approaching as a mentor can only serve you well. As you learn about her career and her style, you will be gathering valuable information to support your career plans and development. And, when you decide to approach her to be your mentor, you will be prepared to refer to what you know about her and make appropriate requests during the interview.

Identifying a woman she admired, doing her homework, and following through on her mentor's suggestions helped Kinsey make a major move in her career.

KINSEY'S AND JACKIE'S STORY

Kinsey was Jackie's boss's administrative support person when she approached Jackie and asked if she would mentor her through a career transition, moving from nonexempt to exempt within the same organization. For over a year Kinsey had observed and admired how Jackie managed her job as a product line manager in marketing. Jackie had a solid reputation as a top performer and as an advocate for women's place in the organization's future. Kinsey had a different educational background and skill base from Jackie, but Kinsey had confidence in her ability to learn and deliver. The two got together, and Jackie agreed to meet with Kinsey and review her goals and approach.

Jackie talked with Kinsey about how she needed to be perceived if she wanted to make the change, and how to make that happen. She suggested what books Kinsey should read, what classes to sign up for, and what events to attend. Then Jackie went around on Kinsey's behalf, networking with her peers to learn about their needs and openings. Kinsey kept up her end of the bargain and worked hard at developing the skills Jackie said she needed if she was to enter the new arena.

A few months later, Jackie heard of an opening for a personnel liaison. The position matched Kinsey's new skills and would give her the exempt position she wanted. Jackie called people she knew and "talked Kinsey up" whenever she had the opportunity. Kinsey did get the position and doesn't hesitate for a minute to thank her mentor and to encourage other women to approach someone they admire for help and support in accomplishing their goals.

As with Kinsey and Jackie, your mentor does not have to be a woman who is doing exactly what you aspire to do. The woman you admire does not have to be a woman with the specific skills or career experiences you need to acquire. She does, though, have to be someone who understands how the organization works and what qualities get someone ahead. Like Jackie, she should be able to guide you in acquiring appropriate skills and experience and should support you as you study and learn. Just as important, she can share with you the story of her ambitions, struggles, and accomplishments, and together you can extract the lessons that apply to your life and goals. Remember, often the greatest gift a woman mentor can offer is her ability to recognize and encourage your talents and powers. A good mentor will mentor you, not recreate herself. She will coach, guide, and encourage you to become the best of yourself.

Is She in the Loop?

This may seem to you to be a harsh and coldly mechanical way to evaluate a potential mentor. After all, there is much more to successful mentoring than providing access and opening doors. However, your potential mentor's connections and willingness to introduce you to influential people can certainly be an important factor in your advancement. If she can send you on challenging assignments and invite you to sit in on important meetings and planning sessions, you will benefit from the visibility and the opportunity to make your own impression within the organization.

A mentor who is "in the loop" can certainly offer you opportunities that someone who is working hard on the sidelines cannot.

If a woman you otherwise admire for her work and achievements eschews connections and is perceived to keep to herself, you may want to be cautious about forming a committed, named, and visible mentoring connection with her. Though she may be admired for her work, she may be perceived as being remote, unapproachable, and destructive to positive team development. Identifying too strongly with her may put you in the same category and isolate you from opportunities. Rather than benefit your career growth, your connection with her could distance you from the action and delay your ambitions. Maintain a friendly connection with her and create mentoring moments where you and she can exchange insights and information, but don't limit yourself to her stewardship. Reach out to others as well.

Values Are Important

Not every woman who is moving up within your profession or organization will be a woman you admire. If she is someone whose approach or tactics you do not admire, she is probably not a good person to seek out as a mentor, even if she is in an influential position and might want a protégé to follow in her path. Question why you hesitate to applaud her achievements. What is it that makes you uncomfortable or unsure about her? Though she seems to be doing something right and moving ahead in your organization, if her values make you uncomfortable—or if she lacks values that you believe are fundamental—she is not a good mentor for you.

Trust your instincts. Don't pursue a mentoring relationship where you already feel uncertainty.

A shared value base is fundamental to a solid, trusting, and honest mentoring relationship. Our values are intrinsic to who we are. Women see in others not isolated functioning entities, but human beings whose behaviors at work, at home, and in the community are integrated into a complex and whole life. Though Shannon may own her own speakers' bureau and be filling bank accounts with her profits, if I am not comfortable with her values (or she with mine), we cannot form an honest, trusting mentoring affiliation. I cannot separate values from accomplishment, and I don't want to. I want a mentor whom I can trust to respect the values of honesty, fairness, and generosity that I see as important in doing business and in living life. When you discover a woman whose accomplishments you admire, before you enthusiastically pursue her as a mentor, observe and investigate her values. We build our lives on our values, and she has built her life and her career on hers. Everything she teaches, her emphasis in coaching, and her guidance and counseling will be infused with her values. If you are uncomfortable with her values, you will be uncomfortable with everything she offers. She will not be a good mentor for you, no matter how successful she has become. She may have skills you admire. You may appreciate the way she can walk up to the president or the CEO at a conference, introduce herself, arrange to meet for coffee in the afternoon, and come away with a contract, but you don't have to connect with her personally to benefit from her talents.

You can observe and extract the skills you admire without forming a personal mentoring relationship. Though she makes contacts with confidence and follows through with competence, you know that the way she treats her consultants is disrespectful and exploitive. You acknowledge her strengths, but you would always have a values conflict. She would not be a good mentor for you.

"A woman has to be very careful that the values and intentions of a potential mentor are in sync with her own," said Gwendolyn, a successful entrepreneur and the first black woman to become president of a formally all white civic organization. "Look at the woman's motivation for mentoring you. Is it so that she can gain recognition and power, or is it a real commitment and investment in you?" Gwendolyn insists that women spend a month or so observing a potential mentor before approaching her with the idea of developing a relationship. This observation period can be vital in finding the "right" mentor.

One thing that gives women a real advantage in finding a mentor is women's ability to read each other well. We can see beneath the surface and know who a person really is, and knowing who a mentor really is and finding a good values match in a mentor are critical. Gwendolyn recalled her first important mentor, Mary. Mary, whom Gwendolyn described as "older, white, and wonderful!" helped mold Gwendolyn in a way that prepared her for work in the public and private sectors. She recommended Gwendolyn for new positions, and she continued to act as a mentor while Gwendolyn went back to school and eventually to public sector work. "What made it work," Gwendolyn made clear, "was a mutual understanding of what a woman has to do to get there and stay (we were both single mothers when we met), and a mutual understanding of what we valued as excellence."

One profession that encourages young professionals to grow through the pairing of experienced people and students new to the field is teaching. And values matches are fundamental to making these relationships work. "For the student-teacher relationship to work best," Deanna, a master art teacher told me, "there must be a shared value base. Those students, you could call them protégés, with whom I have had more than just an instructor-learner relationship have been young teachers who see that we share values. Their style of teaching, their individual strengths and talents may be very different from mine, but we bring to the relationship a commitment to students and a respect for art and teaching that keeps us together." For women in the workplace and the professions today, finding a mentor who shares your values, even if you may have different strengths and skill sets, can form the foundation for a satisfying learning relationship.

A shared understanding of what a woman needs to do to "get there" in the highly competitive business world becomes an important values issue for some women of color. These women respect excellence in performance but do not believe they should have to give up their individual and ethnic identity as a prerequisite for "fitting in." Alma is a Latina woman who is a diversity specialist at a western division of a high tech computer company. In her role as coach, Alma encourages international women to come to her for help with specific issues, usually diversity related, to be resolved.

Often they go on to ask Alma for help in identifying a mentor who shares their belief in the value of diversity. These women want to express who they are and the culture from which they come. They respect excellence, but they do not believe that "assimilating into the white male culture" is necessary for excellence. On the contrary, they, like Alma, believe that pressuring women of color to "adjust" fails both the individual and the corporation. Valuable diverse perspectives are lost, and the business loses an advantage. What these women who come to Alma for a mentor want is someone who believes in the value of diversity and who will respect both their individuality and their cultural background.

Alma gave the example of a Latina woman, Linda, who was preparing for an interview in another state. She worried that she needed to buy a new suit, something that would make her "fit in." Her mentor, Maria, assured her that she was being recruited based on her talent and performance. Maria observed that Linda had always dressed appropriately, even if she had chosen a colorful dress and jacket instead of a short-skirted, black Ann Taylor suit. "You will be your best when you are yourself," Maria advised. "Always remember who you are as a Latina. Wear the bright colors, your nice dresses. Be professional, be confident, and above all be yourself."

You won't always have a "culture broker," as Alma describes herself, to go to for a values check on a prospective mentor. However, you have your own powers of observation. As you observe other women, pay particular attention to the values they profess and what their behaviors and choices suggest. "Good mentoring for women at work," said Karen Wedge, director of women's programs and studies at Colorado State University, "is dependent on the two women involved being matched by values." When the choice is yours, seek a woman with values that you respect and that are compatible with yours.

Shared values encourage trust, and trust is the essential foundation for powerful, effective mentoring.

Questions 4, 5, and 6 of the worksheet presented earlier in this chapter, asked you to respond to different facets of the same issue. Essentially, I am asking you if you feel an affinity with the woman you would like to have as your mentor. Popular research tells us, and my experience and conversations bear this out, that females put a great value on relationship. A "relationship" involves individuals who know each other as people, individuals who have formed a human connection. A relationship involves mutual caring and sharing. From the playground on, females seek friendships based on personal connection. Males can more easily connect around things and activities, such as who has what equipment to bring to the field or who has the batting skills to help win the game. Girls, and then women, want to be with people we like—and want to be liked by the people we are with. Liking and being liked on the job appears to be of greater importance to women than to men. Liking others and being liked at work contributes significantly to a woman's job satisfaction and commitment to her organization or professional location.

Often we realize we like someone when we experience a spontaneous understanding with that other person. Perhaps you both laugh at the same moment during a meeting or respond similarly to speculations about a new product. You respond positively to her values and feel at ease with her style. You recognize that you and she are on the same wavelength.

I once had the possibility of working on a thesis project with a woman I admired for her wonderful intelligence, her scholarship, her professionalism, and her balanced commitment to the academic community and to her family. She had the reputation and connections to support someone interested in an academic career. Though we approached each other with respect and good intentions, we did not share a mutual understanding. To use a common expression, we could not each read where the other was coming from. It was as if we spoke different languages and our messages slid past each other without finding a receptive landing place. It was no fault of either of ours, we were simply on different trajectories and couldn't connect. Appreciation and admiration were there; spontaneous understanding was not. I spent our sessions trying to establish a point of ease. I didn't know when it would be appropriate to laugh or to interject a personal story. I felt constantly on guard and outside myself. Self-consciousness like that precludes relaxed authenticity. Rather than spend the next year straining to make both of us feel comfortable, I thanked her for her time with my thesis proposal and said I needed to reevaluate my enthusiasm for the project—which was true. The connection ended amicably, and with relief on both our parts, I am sure.

When we sense a fundamental understanding with another woman, we are encouraged to be ourselves, to be authentic. A foundation of liking—and being liked—will give your mentoring connection a base from which trust and the genuine will grow. A potential mentor whom you admire, who can give you opportunities and introductions, and who has the skills you need and the values you respect may not be the one for you if you don't spontaneously understand and like each other. You both may try, out of respect and good intentions, but if the affinity isn't there, the inclination to give and the willingness to receive will be strained. It will probably be better for both of you to back off politely, respectful of each other's time and personal energy.

Perhaps in the future mutually appreciative working connections may lead to a more personal connection, and a fulfilling, giving mentoring relationship may evolve. Until then, your role as a protégé is best played where you can be fully receptive to the gifts your mentor has to offer. You will find such a person, and together you will experience a mentoring relationship that benefits both of you in an appreciative, respectful, career- and life-enhancing connection.

Asking a Woman to Mentor You

Life would so easy if just as you committed yourself to finding a mentor, one of the senior officers of your company were to come along and say, "Stacy, I have noticed your performance as leader on the Madison project. I see great potential in you. I like your style and your brains, and I would like to become your mentor." You have been observing her performance, doing research on her career, and talking with others about her style and reputation. You admire what she represents and what she has achieved, and you are prepared and delighted to accept her gesture.

Such things do happen. However, with women in the workplace as busy as we are with our own careers and lives, you cannot expect every successful senior woman who notices and admires your performance to ask to be your mentor. Instead, you as the prospective protégé often have to take the initiative and ask her. Let your personal style and the rapport the two of you have already developed be your guide when you approach your designated mentor with the big question. Remember the story of Kaia and Darcy that began Chapter 4? Kaia used an E-mail message to ask if Darcy would review Kaia's notes in preparation for a performance evaluation interview. Kaia's request for a specific-purpose mentoring session evolved into a successful and productive, ongoing, named but informal mentoring relationship.

You too can take the initiative in establishing a mentoring relationship that will benefit your future and connect you in a vested community of women helping and learning from one another to be our best.

The First Approach

You have done your homework. You know the specifics of Zoe's education, training, and career history. You have observed her in action or followed her performance through network feedback or company newsletters. You know something of her work style and how she manages her time. Now you are ready to ask her for a few minutes to talk with you. You could call and request a few minutes in her office at a time convenient to her, or you could invite her for coffee, for lunch, or to meet for dinner if you are on a business trip together. Personally, I resist cold calls from someone I barely know or don't know at all asking if I will meet her and give her information and direction in establishing a business or writing a book. The approach seems demanding and does not bode well for mutuality and reciprocity. I prefer a face-to-face meeting where we can both be prepared and where we can assess each other's values and affinity, important considerations in the future of a mentoring relationship.

What should you discuss at this first meeting? Be direct and up-front about your intentions. Tell Zoe what you have admired about her and how you believe you could learn from her in a mentoring connection. Include in your conversation specific references to experiences you may have had working together and/or specific traits and accomplishments of hers that you have noticed and admired. Give her your résumé and mention the specific goals you have for your career and for the mentoring opportunity. You may want to give her a written copy of your goals, including questions about what direction you might take in achieving them. This will be good evidence of your commitment to being prepared and ready for action. Talk about how you see mentoring as a working concept. Ask her for stories from her experience as a protégé or mentor. Make it clear that you will be respectful of her time and her job priorities, even suggesting when and how often you would like to call or meet. Discuss the degree of formality that feels comfortable for both of you, and consider suggesting a time frame for the relationship.

Anticipating an end can make the final good-bye and thank you easier for both of you. You might bring along an article that relates to one of her projects or ideas, evidence that you see the mentoring relationship as mutually supportive. Don't pressure her into an immediate response. Leave the meeting or lunch with plans to talk again at a specific time about her decision to become your mentor.

Follow up your meeting with a thank-you note—and with another article, book, or video that relates to something you two discussed. When you call or meet again, be prepared with more questions and with suggestions for scheduling your conversations together.

It is important for you to remember that a potential mentor may have to reject your request. This may have nothing to do with her evaluation of you, but with the mentor's circumstances. Perhaps she is declining the request because of her own work pressures, because of commitments to other protégés, or because she honestly believes she doesn't have enough experience with mentoring to take on the responsibility. In the August 1996 issue of *Working Woman* magazine, Stephen M. Pollan and Mark Levine present a flowchart that guides a prospective protégé through the process of approaching a potential mentor. The flowchart includes the introductory icebreaker, the pitch, three possible response scenarios, and the final expression of thanks that the protégé should offer. If your selected mentor is concerned about time constraints or defers to someone who she thinks could better serve you, Pollan and Levine suggest that you allay her concerns by promising to limit contact time and press the point that she is just the person whose skills and experience you admire and need.

If she is not interested or cannot mentor you at this time, retreat gracefully and say, "Thank you for being direct." When she accepts, make your appreciation clear!

Evaluating Your Mentor

A mentoring relationship is a commitment of time, responsibility, and personal energy—both for you and for your mentor. In a named and acknowledged mentoring relationship, you have identified yourself with a person who has tremendous influence on your choices and on how you are perceived within your work group, corporation, or profession. You should feel comfortable in the relationship and confident of the fact that having a mentor, and this particular mentor, is good for your life and good for your career. If you are not convinced that the connection is working for your advantage and/or your mutual advantage, it is time to end the relationship and say good bye.

If you aren't sure that the mentoring connection is working for you but you haven't identified just why, asking yourself the questions in this worksheet may help focus your concerns. If you have established enough trust and appreciation for mutual learning in your mentoring relationship, you may consider sharing these questions with your mentor. Your responses can show why it is best to end the relationship—or how you can work together to build benefits for both of you into the connection.

Even if you discover that some elements of an ideal mentoring relationship are missing in your situation, the positive factors that are present may be enough to make continuing the relationship a definite benefit for you and your mentor. You're the judge.

	Yes	I'm not sure	No
1. Do you feel that your mentor has respect for your abilities and your potential?	❏	❏	❏

If your answer to this question is no, you may not be getting the attention and opportunities that your mentor would offer if she had more respect for your potential. Perhaps someone else who does appreciate your competence and talents would make a more committed and productive mentor for you.

| 2. Has your mentor kept her commitments? Has your mentor been faithful to your meeting schedule and provided you with the feedback and developmental activities you had agreed would be the focus for your mentoring arrangement? | ❏ | ❏ | ❏ |

	Yes	I'm not sure	No

If she repeatedly cancels her scheduled meetings with you, you have to question her commitment to your relationship. You are wasting time if you prepare for a mentoring session and then nothing happens, as timely feedback can be vital to your career progress. And while you are waiting for her to find you challenging assignments, others are getting the opportunities and the experience. If your mentor is not keeping her commitment to you and to the relationship, let her know of your concern. If she is simply too busy or uninterested, let her tell you so. Thank her for the time she did spend, and end the relationship. You will both be free to pursue activities that better serve your needs and your future.

3. Has your mentor been willing to coach you in the skills you need, or to identify for you where you can acquire those skills?   ❐   ❐   ❐

If you have been in a mentoring relationship for a while and your mentor has not been able to coach you in the skills you need, she may either not have the skills you thought she had, not have the skills to coach you, or not be interested in having you acquire what you need to succeed. Perhaps there is someone else who can and is willing!

4. Is your mentor able to listen to you, hear what you are saying, and accept your point of view even if it is different from her own?   ❐   ❐   ❐

If you feel that your mentor has her own agenda and is not really attentive to your issues and needs, you may be wasting your time. Perhaps she wants to develop a clone, not the unique person you are. It may be the time to detach and look elsewhere.

5. Is your mentor able to identify barriers to your advancement, see solutions to your challenges, and focus on potential opportunities for you?   ❐   ❐   ❐

	Yes	I'm not sure	No

A good mentor is a good sounding board. She should be in a position to see solutions to the problems you face and to identify opportunities that will help get you around the roadblocks on the way to your goals. If she can only warn you about pitfalls and barriers, not offer solutions, she is not helping you. You don't need another person with whom to commiserate about your problems. Your spouse or friends can do that. You want your mentor to be someone who will help you surmount them!

6. Has your mentor functioned as your advocate, introducing you to people who can help your career and sponsoring you for opportunities within your organization or profession? ☐   ☐   ☐

If your mentor has not identified herself with you to the point that others recognize her as your promoter, something may be causing her to hesitate. Is she concerned about the "weak women" connection? Or is she ambivalent about your readiness and, therefore, reluctant to take a chance promoting you in a public way? Find out why she hasn't been more open about your mentoring relationship. If you sense that she will not be the supporter/promoter you need, consider finding someone who believes in you and will happily function as your advocate!

7. Has your mentor been open with you about her own ambitions and developing responsibilities and successes? ☐   ☐   ☐

If your mentor has not chosen to share with you what she is learning, you may have reason to be concerned that she sees you as not an ally but instead as a potential threat and competitor. Bring up what you know of her recent accomplishments and ask why she has not shared them with you. If her answer seems protective and defensive, be concerned that your relationship is not reciprocal, healthy, or productive. If she sees you as potential competition,

	Yes	I'm not sure	No

she could turn from being a supportive mentor to being a "toxic mentor"—one who will do you more damage than good.

8. Has your mentor taken credit for your good ideas or contrbutions without acknowledging you?   ☐   ☐   ☐

If you answer to this one, you should seriously question the integrity and intentions of your mentor. Though she may be superior to you in the hierarchy of your organization, this does not give her the ethical right to present your ideas or your work as her own. Don't let the issue go. Without being threatening, ask her why she didn't include you when she was presenting the progress report to the board. Perhaps a review of your mutual responsibilities in the mentoring relationship will solve the problem. If her response is unsatisfactory to you, you might be better off detaching from the relationship and bringing your ideas directly to your boss or work group without sharing them with your mentor first.

How to Leave Your Mentor

If your responses to the mentor evaluation questions tell you that it is time to end the connection, then it is your responsibility to yourself and to your mentor to take action. Some mentoring connections serve a purpose for a while, and then run out of steam. Even mentoring relationships that have been rewarding for both the protégé and the mentor can eventually wear out their usefulness when you have learned what you can from your mentor and the relationship stalls. However, without a clear end to the mutual responsibilities of the protégé and mentor, the women involved can find themselves dragging through useless hours trying to find something to focus on or to discuss. In such instances, you and your mentor may be taking up unnecessary hours rehashing the same old stuff, or, as Judith

Briles, president of the Briles group and author of *The Confidence Factor,* says, "burping up the same old stuff."

With a no-name relationship, the protégé can just fade away, calling less often and planning fewer lunches or get-togethers. In an informal, named, or assigned relationship, however, "to fade out is a cop-out," as Madeleine Condit, partner in Korn/Ferry International, puts it. Anticipating the end of the mentoring relationship should be part of what you talk about during the mentoring process, even as early as your first mentoring session.

Having discussed the eventuality of an end may make ending the relationship easier when the moment comes. Without that preparation, ending the relationship may take a bit more determination—and tact. If you and your mentor have worked according to a contract or written guidelines, you can refer to the objectives and time limits you established and use this reference to show that you have achieved what you set out to accomplish. You then thank your mentor for all she has contributed to your career and goals.

When you make it clear that you will no longer be coming to her as a protégé, you are relieving her of any residual sense of obligation to reserve time and prepare for your mentoring sessions together. Just because she is no longer your formal mentor, however, does not mean that all elements of the connection are severed. Your former mentor can become part of the personal network you can go to for moments of wisdom and guidance. You can say good bye to her as a mentor, but you can keep her as a member of your personal board of directors!

Saying good bye to your mentor can also mean saying hello to a friend. If you are ending a mentoring relationship because you are taking a new career direction, or perhaps because you have been promoted to a level comparable to that of your previous mentor, you can still continue the trust, appreciation, and sharing that you built during your mentoring years. The boundaries and responsibilities will change when you have passed the formal mentoring stage, but the gifts of wisdom and caring can continue as you enjoy a growing and expanding friendship.

If You Want to Learn More

Bramson, Robert M., Ph.D. *Coping with Difficult People* (New York: Dell Publishing, 1981).

Furnham, Adrian F. *Personality at Work: The Role of Individual Differences in the Workplace* (New York: Routledge, 1994).

Goleman, Daniel. *Emotional Intelligence: Why it can matter more than IQ* (New York: Bantam Books, 1995).

Tieger, Paul D., and Barbara Barron-Tieger. *The Art of Speed Reading People: Harness the Power of Personality Type and Create What You Want in Business and in Life* (Boston: Little, Brown, 1998).

Weisinger, Hendrie Davis, Ph.D. Susan Williams, editor. *Emotional Intelligence at Work: The Untapped Edge for Success* (San Francisco: Jossey-Bass Publishers, 1997).

CHAPTER 7

Protecting Your Protégé/Mentor Relationship

LAURALYN'S STORY

My daughter Lauralyn is a TV news journalist in an early stage of her career. As she was traveling around the country visiting TV stations, she met Jacque, a Denver-area news editor, and Celeste, an eastern-market TV news reporter. Both women, after meeting and talking with Lauralyn, spontaneously offered to be available to her as informal mentors. They are not in a position to hire Lauralyn, but they have knowledge and experience of the TV news industry that has been and will be valuable to Lauralyn as her career progresses. Celeste has shared stories of woman-to-woman interactions within the industry. She has been blunt about how a woman must maintain an attractiveness/credibility balance, and how Lauralyn should prepare to confront the competition, jealousy, and sabotage that women can encounter in this profession. Celeste has provided more than stories and a sounding board for Lauralyn. She has read over résumés and cover letters and provided feedback on tapes that Lauralyn has sent for critique.

Jacque and Celeste, true to their promises, have been great resources for coaching, guidance, and insider tips as Lauralyn pursues her career. Lauralyn, in turn, has honored their generosity by keeping them informed of her activities and letting them know how their suggestions have helped her develop skills and gain experience. Jacque and Celeste have made themselves available as an ongoing resource for Lauralyn. Their relationship is friendly, but fundamentally professional.

In a very different context, Lauralyn and Lisa Janssen have been friends since elementary school. While Lauralyn went to Japan and taught with the Japanese Exchange and Teaching (JET) program for two years after college, Lisa graduated from Harvard Business School and is now a senior analyst in strategic planning for the Walt Disney Company in Los Angeles. They have chosen different career directions, and though their friendship comes first, they often find themselves acting as mentors for each other as they face job decisions and career-related challenges. They don't use the word *mentoring* when asking for help in working through a issue with a coworker or for coaching before a presentation, but the focus within their relationship shifts.

"When I say to Lisa, please give me some help with this," Lauralyn says, "I can feel the tone of our conversation change into another mode. Lisa becomes professionally directed, offering me honest feedback and gritty, no-holds-barred coaching. Lisa trusts me when I ask for serious, honest mentoring on negotiating my way through organizational levels, and I trust Lisa when she wants honest feedback about her peer interactions and team skills."

When friends ask each other to step into a mentoring role, they are giving each other permission to be direct, objective, and honest. Friends mentoring friends never lose touch with the trust and respect that underlies their relationship. They take the request for mentoring seriously and make an honest effort to provide information and insights that will support their friend in reaching her goals.

You can't completely separate friendship from mentoring. You don't want to be formal and professional with each other always, but during the mentoring sessions, you change the rules. You say, in effect, "Be absolutely honest with me, even if you feel uncomfortable being critical or suggesting a direction you know I don't want to go. Don't put my feelings first right now, but give me the information and advice I need to get through this situation." "The difference," Lauralyn says, "in being mentored by a friend instead of an informal or formal mentor is that we know each other so well, we can laugh when the ambitious career focus becomes too intense. Laughing doesn't make the mentoring any less serious, but it helps us keep a healthy perspective on the importance of career and the importance of the personal and whole-life issues we have always shared as friends."

Protecting the Mentoring Experience

Mentoring connections, like friendships and all relationships, require respect and attention if they are to survive. Your relationship with your mentor has great gifts to offer. You can protect the potential of that gift exchange by preparing to protect your mentoring relationship from some of the threats that have troubled woman-to-woman mentoring pairs in the past. You and your mentor can become a model for other women, and you can share the positive experience with your protégés in the future.

Managing the Friendship Issue

Friends can become mentors for each other, but should protégés and mentors become friends? Mentoring connections that begin in a career- or work-related context have a different base from those relationships that begin as spontaneous, affinity friendships. You have selected your career mentor because of her reputation and position, or she has sought you out because of the potential she has noted in your work-related performance. You come together with a work-related agenda, and your respect for professionalism in your relationship should honor that commitment.

With good female emphasis, you and your mentor like and respect each other. You are trusting and authentic, and you willingly reveal your frustrations as well as your aspirations. When women come together in a mentoring relationship based on affinity and caring, nurture and support, the connection often mirrors the beginning of a friendship. But be careful. Even with informal mentoring connections, and definitely with formal relationships, when the context is the workplace, the focus is, and should be, profes-

sional. The help and information exchanged in a mentoring relationship should relate first to your work and then to your work as it
affects and is integrated into your life goals and rewards.

Having friendship expectations for a work-connected mentoring relationship can doom the professional opportunity and leave
you, or both of you, hurt, angry, and discouraged.

Maintaining boundaries of intimacy in a mentoring relationship can contribute to a satisfying experience for both the protégé
and the mentor. To be a successful protégé often means respecting
the professional boundaries your mentor sets up to protect her vulnerability as well as yours.

Debra Benton, a management consultant and author of *Lions
Don't Have to Roar, How to Think Like a CEO*, and *$100,000 Club*,
sees friendship and mentoring as two distinctly different relationships. "Mentoring is strictly business," Benton says. "You have to
keep the intimate stuff out."

Intimacy and the nature of that intimacy is what makes friendship an issue for women in mentoring relationships. When women
are drawn to relationships and to one another through affinity and
a sharing of values, when they become vested in one another's
lives, this feels to many of us like friendship. Psychotherapist Anne
Wilson Schaef, in her classic book, *A Woman's Reality*, describes
female friendships. "For women," she says, "the focus of friendship is verbal intimacy and mutual sharing of one's being. True
friends are those who totally expose themselves to each other, sure
in the knowledge that to do so is safe."

The problem that friendship can pose for mentoring relationships is determining how much of that mutual sharing of intimacy
is "safe" and comfortable for the two people involved. Sometimes,
one person, let's say the protégé, is much more comfortable sharing
intimacies and personal facts, such as anecdotes about family life
or health problems, than the other person is, and this can create
tension and conflicts. Will your mentor's knowing that you are re-
covering from an abusive relationship or have been treated for de-
pression affect her professional assessment of your potential or your
ability to handle constructive coaching and tough assignments?

Knowing that your mentor is lonely or needful in her personal life, for example, could naturally lead many women to want to provide the company and caring that her mentor needs. The focus of the relationship could then easily shift from work- and career-related issues to the personal obligations and care-taking expectations of a conventional female friendship.

The objectivity a mentor can provide, albeit with caring and friendliness, can be lost in the up-closeness of tears and stories shared over Coke and potato chips in front of late-night TV. After such intimacy, harsh criticism of your meeting-management skills can become more difficult for your mentor if she fears hurting your feelings or making you withdraw. And you as the protégé could lose professional respect for your mentor and tend to dismiss her assignments and challenges if you keep remembering how out of control she seems to be in her personal relationships. Even though her career wisdom may be excellent and on target, you will have a difficult time keeping the professional and personal circumstances separate. And the effectiveness of her mentoring will diminish.

If you have any doubts about the appropriateness of intimate sharing within a business relationship, don't share.

You can still enjoy a rewarding and connected relationship as a learning team without burdening each other with your vulnerabilities.

In her article "Rules of Power and Familiarity in Faculty Mentor/Graduate Student Relationships," Vickie Rutledge Shields got to the essence of the friendship dilemma for many women in work and professional situations. Although in most cases there will be a hierarchical difference between the protégé and her mentor, she explained, there will also be an interweaving of power and familiarity that can provide "very difficult distractions."

"Once a friendship is established," Shields wrote, "with a faculty mentor, particularly a woman mentor, a female graduate student is inclined to nurture and maintain that relationship. One way to do this is by making herself vulnerable to her friend, sharing very personal information about herself while learning equally intimate information about her mentor. The two may do favors for one another outside of work, therefore 'owing' one another in informal ways."

The women may also ritualize their friendship by sharing intimate gossip, often about others with whom they work. If power were equal, these behaviors would represent fairly typical female friendship patterns. In the protégé/mentor relationship, however, power is never really equal. The protégé can be caught off guard when her mentor makes decisions that go against an interest or desire that she has shared or when she herself has to take an action that she knows will hurt her mentor and her mentor's wishes for her. "Vulnerability already exists in this relationship, and this turn of events can lead to a sense of betrayal and even abandonment," Shields wrote. This betrayal can be felt by the protégé or by the mentor.

Whether or not to be friends with women at work is one of the dilemmas that young women face, especially in the closeness of a mentoring connection. "Women protégés may expect different things from women mentors, such as frequent nurturing and acceptance, and may become extremely disappointed when these are absent or provided to a lesser degree than desired," wrote Parker and Kram in their article "Women Mentoring Women." Junior women often expect their female mentors to be more empathetic to their struggles than male mentors, as well as more patient and available to provide support and counsel.

Problems can arise, however, when senior women don't accept or don't understand the assumptions of their junior protégés. If the senior women have had male mentors, they may have learned to emphasize the coaching and sponsorship elements of a mentoring relationship and to "de-emphasize such psychosocial functions as counseling and friendship." The different perspectives of the junior and senior women on the nature and demands of friendliness and friendship in the mentoring relationship can leave both parties confused, unsatisfied, and even angry. Talking about the possible conflicts early in the mentoring relationship can help. You and your mentor can agree on boundaries for sharing and caring. Though it is difficult to anticipate what intimacies could lead to conflict, you can agree, for example, to limit your sharing of vulnerabilities and fears to those that affect your attitude and commitment at work.

The nature of woman-to-woman mentoring is that it invites and allows us to share our frustrations and worries with a person who can relate to our lives. Managing what we share and how we express our struggles and needs is a challenge for all of us in a mentoring relationship based on affinity and caring. Another element of the relationship, however, is respect. Respect for your mentor and for the opportunity provided by your mentoring connection should be your guide in maintaining the balance between authentic sharing of our real and professional concerns and compromising ourselves with self-abasing intimacies and confessions.

"Everyone I have mentored has become my friend," a woman in city government told me, "but I was their mentor first. When they were my protégés, we kept the relationship focused on career and goals. We shared trust and affection, but we respected the boundaries of a workplace relationship—and we were successful together."

Remembering That Your Mentor Isn't Your Mother

If some women face a challenge separating mentoring from friendship, other women have perhaps the greater challenge of separating mentoring from mothering.

You may be a woman for whom the idea of forming a constructive, supportive learning alliance with a woman in a superior position is fraught with high anxiety, resistance, and even fear. Though I am not a psychologist, I have done enough reading and listening to appreciate the enormous influence our relationships with our mothers have on our relationships with other women. "The mother/daughter relationship is one of the most intense relationships a

111

woman ever experiences," wrote Julie and Dorothy Firman in *Daughters & Mothers: Healing the Relationship*.

> It is strong and it is primary. Although your mother may no longer be part of your daily life, you still carry her with you, for better or for worse. This first and essential relationship has a powerful, though often subtle, effect upon your current dealings with your mate, children, friends, and *yourself*, for without thinking about it, or even knowing it, we are bound and conditioned by our pasts—and most deeply, by the mother/daughter relationship.

Louise Eichenbaum and Susie Orbach, in their book *Between Women*, add that "Women relating to each other see not just their friends or colleagues, they project onto them a whole range of emotions that reflect the legacy of their relationships with their mothers."

Fundamental to establishing a sound, constructive relationship with a female mentor is understanding that she is *not* your mother. She has not shared your history with your mother, and she does not want to play the role of your mother.

You and your mentor should come together as mature, independent women extending yourselves to give to and learn from each other in a mature, growth-focused relationship. Women who have grown up with trustworthy, strong, empowering, supportive mothers will bring those expectations and their respect for women to a comfortable and productive woman-to-woman mentoring experience.

If you have an unspecified ambivalence about joining in a learning relationship with a senior or superior woman, you could be denying yourself an occasion for enhanced growth and increased life satisfaction. It could be that unresolved issues in your relationship with your mother are interfering with your ability to connect positively with older, accomplished women at work. Use the following worksheet to focus your feelings about your mother and how your relationship with her may be affecting your expectations for relationships with other women. Take time to think about and learn from your answers. The questions are general and wide open, but the reasons why you agree or disagree may be quite specific and vivid. Assure yourself that even if you missed having a trusting, honest, and secure relationship with your mother, you are not barred from establishing a productive, mutually appreciative, and empowering connection with a woman mentor. The better you understand your background and expectations, the more control you have over what you can offer and receive as a receptive and appreciative protégé.

Inventory	Agree	Not Sure	Disagree
1. My mother is honest in her communications with me.	❐	❐	❐
2. My mother is someone I trust to protect my best interests.	❐	❐	❐
3. My mother's criticisms are constructive and caring, not destructive and cruel.	❐	❐	❐
4. My mother recognizes and supports my talents and strengths.	❐	❐	❐
5. My mother wants to see me advance and succeed.	❐	❐	❐

Gaining insight into your relationship with your mother may help you identify factors that are impeding your mature relationships with women who can add great value to your life. The books listed at the end of this chapter can further help you understand and gain control of destructive patterns and benefit from genuine, constructive relationships.

Respecting Different Choices

When you seek to be mentored by a woman, you are seeking to be enhanced by her wisdom and her experience. It is natural for many of us be drawn to a woman mentor because of the common bond we share as women. We seek and expect understanding on issues concerning being a woman, and we value the potential of our relationships, specifically our woman-to-woman mentoring connections, on that premise. However, it is just this expectation of identification and understanding from another woman that can precipitate deep fissures in our relationships and can potentially divide us and leave us angry and disillusioned.

Alexis, a young CPA I spoke with, admired her assigned mentor, Twila, but could never be completely open and honest with Twila about her hopes for a family. Twila had chosen career over children and family and was, after a brief marriage, staunchly single and proudly self-sufficient. Alexis saw Twila's position as critical of her own and withdrew from any personal discussion of family and career to protect "our feelings."

For many women, work/career and lifestyle choices are so fraught with emotional sensitivity and protectiveness that when we cannot include our feelings on these subjects in a relationship, we are incomplete—and so is the relationship.

Some of us become extremely sensitive about our personal decisions concerning having children, for example, and how we will integrate our career and family priorities. Though we may expect other women to share our needs and choices, we know that caring, thoughtful women make decisions that are different from ours. As protective of our decisions as some of us are, we sometimes conclude that for a woman to make different life decisions from ours means that she is critical of our priorities. Taken to the extreme, some of us conclude that if her decisions are different from ours, she rejects our validity and our value. To avoid the pain of criticism and difference, some avoid the issue of personal commitments entirely in their mentoring relationships. When this happens, the relationship becomes compartmentalized and objectified, and both women miss being able to probe the deep life issues that affect their goals, work commitment, job satisfaction and wholeness. The mentoring becomes functional and routine, with much of the richness that characterizes woman-to-woman relationships lost. Our careers may gain, but our sense of being known and our ability to give of our whole selves is diminished.

Kathy Kram, Boston University professor, researcher, and expert on mentoring, and her associate Victoria A. Parker addressed this challenge in their article "Women Mentoring Women: Creating Conditions for Connection," in the March/April, 1993, issue of *Business Horizons* magazine.

> Paradoxically, the common experiences women share in the workplace, which are the attraction and glue for a mentoring relationship, often remain indiscussible in a junior-senior pairing and therefore substantially limit the potential value of the alliance for both parties. In relationships between women at different career stages, self-disclosure, active listening, and feedback often tend to be strangely absent.

They concluded by observing that:

> Junior women who perceive senior women of an earlier generation as having made different choices may fear both having to make such a choice and being judged for making a different choice. Senior women may be envious of junior women's expanded choices and fear they are being harshly judged for choices made in a different era.

Though openness about personal choices and individual situations can be an important factor in forming solid mentoring connections between two women, a mutual understanding of values and priorities remains fundamental for a mentoring relationship to work. Jane Chestnutt, editor-in-chief of *Woman's Day* magazine, is a gracious and confident woman. I spoke with Jane in her New York office. Early in our conversation she made it clear that for her a woman's performance at work is what counts for her advancement and success, not her personal choices. Though Jane offers that she has no children, for her the focus in a business context is, and should be, how this individual is performing her work.

Each individual has her perspective and her style, and when you look for a mentor, values, priorities and personal styles all become important considerations. For many of us, our commitment choices weigh significantly in our women-to-women relationships, whether the relationship is between good friends or a protégé and her mentor.

Rather than avoiding the issue and remaining uncomfortable, you, as a protégé, should be willing to include your personal goals in conversations with your mentor. You should listen empathetically to your mentor's stories of her struggles with these decisions. What you will share in this exchange are the issues of a woman's life, the gifts of our mutual and individual experiences. From knowing and being known, from growing respect for the depth and dimension of our lives, we become vested in the power of our mutual future.

At the 1995 Summit on Women's Economic Security held in Denver, Colorado, Hillary Rodham Clinton gave the keynote address. On the general subject of women criticizing the commitment choices of other women, she admonished her audience to stop pointing fingers and to start holding out helping hands.

Women criticizing other women for being different from themselves is a challenge with the potential to divide us as women working together. For protégés and mentors, commitment differences can impede honest disclosure of the deepest issues affecting a woman's career and life success. Talking through our feelings and experiences will help us get beyond the conflict to a place where we can, with trust and honesty, learn and grow together.

Anticipating Competition

"I knew Marla was good, very good, when I agreed to mentor her," Colleen, an account executive, told me about her protégé. "We talked about the fact that we might end up competing for the same vice presidency, especially in view of the downsizing our company had been experiencing. My belief is that being a mentor means preparing someone to fly, helping her realize her full potential. If that means she will be competing with me, I understand. I won't like it that my own career may stand still, but I will take pride in what I was able to help her accomplish."

Would that all your mentors had Colleen's attitude. Colleen made it easy for her protégés to discuss with her the potential for competition and to prepare for how they will respond if such circumstances occur.

Competition is not an easy subject for many women to discuss, and, as a result, we can suffer considerable pain when we have to confront competing with others whom we have looked up to, respected, and followed.

When an aspiring woman identifies an accomplished and high performing woman to mentor her, the difference in status and experience between the women defines the relationship. The younger or less experienced woman defers to the status of her senior adviser and guide. She is the superior one, the teacher, the professional mother. But as the protégé gains in knowledge and experience, the possibility that the two women could end up competing against each other enters the equation.

What will you as a protégé do when it becomes clear that you may soon be in competition with your mentor? With downsizing, consolidation, and specialization, the levels between you and your mentor may be compressed, and you may find yourself identified as a contender for a position your mentor has held or has been preparing for herself.

Some protégés heading toward competition with their mentors respond like a daughter who feels wrong competing with her mother. I have seen protégés in this situation choose to avoid the awkwardness and challenge by backing off. Some stifle their own ambitions and put their energy into supporting their mentor's cause. Others hide from their mentor, disconnecting without acknowledging an end to the relationship. This approach can create tension and distrust between the original mentoring pair that is quickly picked up by the workplace grapevine. Confidence in the protégé's trustworthiness and the consistency of her commitment comes into question, and her chances of finding another high performer as a mentor are diminished—along with her chances of being elevated to a position of greater responsibility and influence.

A more constructive approach to the competition issue is for you as the protégé to consider the possibility that you and your mentor have similar long term goals and that, given the scarcity of positions at the top, you may at some point be in competition. This possibility may affect the trust and information sharing that can be so valuable in a protégé/mentor connection. However, talking openly about competition may also lead to honest sharing about how women can better prepare ourselves and cooperate with others in a competitive workplace.

Together, you and your mentor may come to an understanding about each woman's right to challenge herself to top performance and agree to cooperate in encouraging each other to be her best. Your mentor may be the one who wants to talk about competition early in your mentoring relationship. She has probably had experience in managing competition and will want to help prepare you to approach your advancement opportunities in a fair, realistic, and professional manner.

Formal mentoring programs often anticipate the competition issue and assign protégés mentors in different functional areas, with whom they are unlikely to find themselves in contention for the same position. You can protect yourself in the same way by selecting a mentor in a noncompeting area or even in another division within your corporation.

The same precaution applies if you are an entrepreneur seeking another small business owner to be your mentor. You can meet wonderful potential mentors at your chamber of commerce small business workshops or other networks, such as National Association of Women Business Owners, that attract successful entrepreneurs. Dr. Courtney Price, author of *101 + Answers to the Most Frequently Asked Questions from Entrepreneurs*, (John Wiley & Sons, 1999) makes the point that "it is essential [that] protégés and mentors in entrepreneurial businesses not be competitors." Though it may seem natural for a woman beginning her career-counseling business to go to an established career counselor and ask to be her mentor, she should not put this pressure on the experienced woman. This would be like asking someone to give you all her information, materials, and clients with nothing in exchange!

Courtney Price talked with me about how she and Jane Applegate, another columnist, have worked out their peer mentor/noncompetitor relationship. "We discovered," Courtney told me, "that though we both work with questions and answers to business questions, I give hard answers and Jane uses anecdotes. We identified how we don't compete, and can go on respecting and mentoring one another."

As owners of a small business, my partners and I are frequently asked for one-time advice sessions by women who want to establish communications training businesses. We are happy to meet and share the story of our partnership, but we advise the women to find a long-term mentor in a field that does not compete with us. We want to share what we've learned and encourage other women. We don't, however, want to give ourselves away to the competition and end up angry with ourselves and resentful of the others involved. I am comfortable exchanging these feelings with a woman who comes to me because I believe in creating the most conducive possible circumstances for rewarding protégé/mentor relationships. When I can, I suggest to her a woman I know in another business area who has a lot to offer and is interested in mentoring promising young women. I like knowing that I have facilitated a connection that will bring growth and rewards to women who appreciate the wisdom and experience women have to offer.

Honoring the Gift

You as a protégé can take a role in anticipating and resolving some of the relationship issues that have the potential to threaten positive and constructive interactions with your mentor. The riches of experience and wisdom that women have to offer women are gifts to be treasured and honored. You can participate in creating a learning connection that brings two women together in a process that enhances learning and development for both of you. And when you can model the power and potential of this connection for other women, you contribute to the finest gift we can give each other—the gift of ourselves toward a strong, caring, and vested future for women and for the workplace that honors all people becoming our best together.

If You Want to Learn More

Barber, Jill, and Rita E. Watson. *Sisterhood Betrayed: Women in the Workplace and the All About Eve Complex* (New York: St. Martin's Press, 1991).

Bassoff, Evelyn S. *Mothers & Daughters: Loving & Letting Go* (New York: NAL/ Dutton, 1988).

Boynton, Marilyn Irwin, and Mary Dell. *Goodbye Mother Hello Woman: Reweaving the Daughter Mother Relationship* (Oakland, Calif.: New Harbinger Publications, 1995).

Cocola, Nancy Wasserman, and Arlene Modica Matthews. *How to Manage Your Mother: Skills and Strategies to Improve Mother-Daughter Relationships* (New York: Simon and Schuster, 1992).

DesRoches, Brian, Ph.D. *Your Boss Is Not Your Mother: Creating Autonomy, Respect, and Success at Work* (New York: William Morrow and Co., Inc., 1995).

Duff, Carolyn S., and Barbara Cohen. *When Women Work Together: Using Our Strengths to Overcome Our Challenges* (Berkeley, Calif.: Conari Press, 1993).

Eichenbaum, Louise, and Susie Orbach. *Between Women* (New York: Viking Press, Inc., 1988).

Firman, Julie, and Dorothy Firman. *Daughters & Mothers: Healing the Relationship* (New York: Crossroad, 1994).

Kram, Kathy E., and Victoria Parker. "Women Mentoring Women Creating Conditions for Connection" *Business Horizons*, March/April 1993, pp. 42–51.

Expanding the Possibilities: Additional Opportunities for Learning From Women

SUSAN'S STORY

Susan, a robust 53-year-old with a husband, two daughters, and a pair of West Highland terriers, heads warehouse operations for a large brewery. Susan never had a female mentor. There were no women above her as she progressed in her career, and today she is the only woman at her level. She has no ongoing mentoring relationships with younger women; however, she is often approached by women from all areas of the brewery operation for information and counsel. And she welcomes their inquiries and respects their confidences.

They want Susan to help guide them on a safe and sure path toward career heights and a life they can live with. Susan seems to have achieved the balance they want, and they come to her seeking wisdom, reassurance, and support. Susan talks with these women and learns about their ambitions and their lives. She then offers to work directly with these women's supervisors to put together meaningful development plans for their futures. The mentoring connections with these junior women are short-term, but Susan feels that her knowledge and experience are extremely valuable to the women she advises. "No man," Susan claims, "would be able to identify the development needs of a woman in a male-dominated industry. I can, and my credibility comes from my visible accomplishments and success."

Susan's way of mentoring, she acknowledges, does not fit the standard definition of a developmental relationship, which includes coaching, counseling, and advocating a protégé over many months, many years, or even a lifetime. She would like to nurture a more traditional mentoring connection, but she doesn't have the time at work or outside of work. What time she does have she spends with her daughters and her husband or on community activities that focus on women's issues. She is adamant that honest, valuable, long-term mentoring takes an emotional and time commitment that she is not in a position to offer. "Someone else will have to play that role," she states. "I do what I can in the short term. Women know I am available, and I appreciate their seeking my input."

Short-Term Mentors

Susan is a short-term mentor, by her own description and by choice. She has experience, knowledge, information, and understanding to offer, and she wants other women to know that she is available. She has built a reputation for giving, and smart women honor her willingness by coming to her for guidance and support. Susan has her limits and makes her terms clear: You come to me prepared with goals and options, or with questions about a woman's place and future in this company. I will help us find a course to follow and project the future as best I can. Then I will help you on your way by meeting with your supervisor and contributing suggestions for your development plan. I cannot be your permanent or exclusive sounding board. I want to be available to other women who seek my help, and I am busy. However, if you want to stop by and let me know how our plan is working and how your life is progressing, I welcome your visit. You can teach me from your experience, and both of us can reach out to women who can benefit from what we have learned.

Women like Susan are available for you. I have been a short-term mentor many times, and I look forward to meeting and sharing what I have learned with more women in the future. It is up to you to ask, to prepare, to share honestly, to listen respectfully, to report back—and to say thank you. We can offer many gifts this way, and, to borrow a phrase, the gifts will keep on giving.

Peer Mentors

Perhaps the woman you would like as your organizational mentor is too busy to mentor you right now, and the Susan of your company is leaving for a five-year assignment in Brazil. To add to your frustrations, your company has no formal mentoring program for you to enter, and your professional network has two hundred interested protégés and six women who have volunteered to mentor. No one seems to be available to provide the work-related reality check, the information hot line, the performance feedback, and the emotional support that could be of such value.

"Instead of waiting for the perfect mentor to come along," Marjorie Vincent of Oasis Communications said in an interview with *Executive Female* magazine, "I encourage women to create their own mentoring network of colleagues and peers." Vincent did not mean to confuse mentoring with networking. Networking involves sharing information about the workplace and job opportunities, but it does not involve the mutual commitment and continuity of peer mentoring. Vincent expects peer mentors to be committed to one another's career success and dedicated to empowering one another. Peer mentors can be confidants, counselors, and coaches for one another. Peers, Vincent believes, can be "especially effective in teaching each other alternative styles of presentation or management, or rehearsing tough confrontations like getting honest feedback from your boss."

Kathy Kram, in her book *Mentoring at Work: Developmental Relationships in Organizational Life*, stated that in peer relationships, the "lack of hierarchical dimension" facilitates "communication, mutual support, and collaboration." Kram spoke directly to the advantages of having a woman-to-woman peer mentoring relationship when she wrote that "female managers at every career stage refer to female peers as providing role modeling or counseling functions that were absent from a mentor relationship with a male senior colleague."

Kram sees peer mentors as being able to share information, strategize together, and offer one another job-related feedback. As the peer relationships evolve and become more personal and committed, the peers can offer one another "confirmation, emotional support, personal feedback and friendship." "Special peers," of which you may have no more than one or two in a lifetime, Kram equates to a best friend. A special peer is a person with whom you can express your "professional dilemmas, vulnerabilities, and individuality." However, even though she may be your special peer and your best work friend, the boundaries for workplace friendships still apply. She may well be your career soul sister, but yours is still a workplace relationship. Until circumstances make it acceptable and safe for you to extend your friendship, respect the boundaries of intimacy and don't burden each other with distracting demands.

In the early years of your career, your peer mentors help you get into the swing by sharing what they observe and what they are learning from their colleagues' experiences and experiments.

Beyond information sharing, your peer mentors can give you encouragement, support, and feedback on what they witness of your performance.

As you grow to know and trust one another, your peers can become valuable sounding boards and resources for your work and family issues.

"Individuals tend to think of developmental relationships as traversing hierarchical lines," wrote Linda Hill of the Harvard Business School. "Such a perspective is, however, extremely limiting, for relationships with peers can also be developmental." What peers cannot offer you, in most cases, is access to influential superiors. And there can be the problem of competition among peers, which discourages some women from seeking a peer mentor. However, in her study of managers, Hill found that for these managers, having access to a network of peers was an important ingredient of a successful workplace experience. "After the new managers overcame some of the inhibitory effects of competitive pressure with peers," she wrote, "peer interactions provided a supportive forum in which they could explore how they thought and felt about the challenges they faced."

Competition with your peer mentors may become a factor if you are on the same career path, especially if your organization rewards individual performance more than team contribution and sound relationship skills. Consider what you and your peers can learn from confronting the competition issue. Is it necessary to distance yourselves from each other, or is it possible to respect each other's potential and become vested in the future of someone whom you want to help succeed? If you are comfortable with the reality of competition, you can continue as valuable mentors for each other. As you share feedback on performance and offer encouragement to excel, you are both learning. You become vested in each other's success. When you move ahead, your peer will know that she had a hand in your accomplishments, and you will recognize your contribution to her success when she advances. Both of you can honor that contribution with continuing support and with commitment to a growing network of women vested in one another's success.

For women at a senior executive level who want a career-focused relationship with another woman, finding a peer mentor may be the only option. At this stage, in the middle years, we find ourselves mentoring younger women but not having the learning dialogue and support of an experienced women for ourselves. High-level women who want a mentor often face a real scarcity of women who are more advanced in the workplace than they and who have time to spend on someone else's career. However, establishing a peer mentoring relationship with a high-level executive may not be as simple as establishing such a relationship at the lower levels. Very few of these women have minutes to spare, and a free lunch hour is more the exception than the rule. "Many senior executives," Marjorie Vincent noted in *Executive Female*, "are turned off by a bald 'I want to be your partner' approach." She suggests cultivating relationships gradually. Figure out how to develop a relationship that will be mutually beneficial. Your peer mentoring at this stage could involve information about options for career challenges, cultivating vision, developing leadership opportunities, and managing life changes and workplace demands. The wisdom that women accumulate is wisdom that we want to share. There are so many ways we can learn and develop together, as individuals and as a community of women learning from one another how to enhance the future for all women.

One of my own experiences with peer mentoring has been with my partner, Betty Brown. Betty and I, along with a third partner, Gail, began BCA Resources, a training, editing, and consulting partnership, in 1983. We had been graduate students and composition instructors together at the local university, and we saw in BCA Resources an opportunity to honor our backgrounds in writing and teaching writing without repeating our pasts as classroom teachers. None of us had been in business before, and each of us came to BCA with different strengths and skills, although we shared a common value base and a commitment to enhancing and empowering one another. We became peer mentors, meeting the mentoring criteria as coaches, sounding boards, encouragers, and counselors. Our understanding of mutual mentoring had a foundation in trust and respect. We critiqued one another's training style, and we learned together about conducting a business. We listened to one another's apprehensions and addressed one another's self-doubts with honest feedback and growth challenges. We supported one another in finding balance in our work and family lives and respected confidentiality about issues affecting our ambitions and our identities. We trusted and respected one another and we grew, as a business and as women. Gail moved to another state, but today Betty and I continue as peer mentors, sharing what we learn, offering what wisdom we have attained, listening and guiding each other through changes in our business and in our life/work balances.

Peer mentoring is well adapted to today's work climate, where the emphasis seems to be increasingly on good performance and work satisfaction and not necessarily on promotion. "For many women today, mentoring isn't about going up," a human resources manager told me. "The issue today is how to keep going day to day and fit into a system women didn't create. Peer mentors can give us the information and encouragement to keep going."

Peer mentoring need not be limited to one-on-one relationships. Tina, an engineer I spoke with in Los Angeles, has found women where she works to be open to peer mentoring because "we prefer to see each other as a team." Women in the informal mentoring teams at her office schedule time to meet and provide the goal setting, feedback, coaching, and listening that happen in formalized hierarchical relationships. "Taking a team approach to mentoring," Tina told me, "has eliminated some of the challenges of competition and hierarchical discomfort that women can face in traditional one-on-one mentoring situations."

Horizontal Mentoring

Your peer mentors will most likely be your own age, or close to your own age. When you become peer mentors, you will most likely be in similar jobs at the same level within your organization. The difference between your peer mentors and your horizontal mentor is that your horizontal mentor will most likely be older than you and will have been on the job long enough to have a background of experience, ctions with others throughout the organization, and a political or cultural savvy that can provide you with important information.

"Gail comes alongside me and helps me get where I want to go," Roe said of her horizontal mentoring relationship with Gail in a city light and power department. Gail, in turn, said of her relationship with Roe: "If Roe's sole intent was to move up in our organization, she would be better off with a male mentor. If she wants freedom to move on a broad base, then I'm a good mentor for her."

Gail and Roe refer to their relationship as mentoring. Gail is older than Roe and more experienced in their field. As a result, she is in a position to give Roe developmental opportunities. In addition, because Roe and Gail are both women, they can discuss family and child-care concerns that Roe is uncomfortable sharing with her immediate supervisor, who might see her concerns as a threat to her reliability. Though Gail is not in a hierarchical position above Roe, she is in a position to provide Roe with skills training and coaching on her image as an excellent performer. For example, Gail was able to re-word Roe's job description to reflect all that Roe was doing and to make her "look good."

What a horizontal mentor can do for you is what Gail has been able to do for Roe. "Though we have different jobs, we are in many ways parallel," Gail explains. "I have had more experience and more years, and with that comes a bit more clout. What I have been able to do for Roe as her horizontal mentor was to give her the information she needs about the organization, and then to provide the breadth she needs to prepare for a vertical move when she is ready."

Your horizontal mentors can give you the information, coaching, and guidance that will enhance your work opportunities and enrich your life. When you reach across, you are extending the connection of women willing and prepared to support each other in achieving a satisfying career and a fulfilling life.

Mentoring Groups

Peer and horizontal mentoring can certainly enhance your career growth and job satisfaction. However, you may still want to benefit from the perspective and wisdom of a more senior, experienced mentor. When your work situation makes it difficult for you to establish a one-on-one mentoring connection with an informed and experienced senior woman, mentoring groups are an exciting and viable alternative. Even if you have the opportunity for one-on-one mentoring, you may find the supportive and growth-directed intent of mentoring groups to be both appealing and rewarding.

A mentoring group brings a group of six to ten women together with a mentor, or mentors, usually two to four management levels above the peers. The members of the circle agree to a meeting schedule and commit themselves to attending the mentoring sessions. A relationship develops among the circle participants in which trust and honesty invite openness and sharing among the mentors and the peers. These circles address a range of work-related issues. The mentor serves as an informed and experienced resource, but all members participate in sharing their experiences, insights, suggestions, and support.

I first read about mentoring groups in the 1993 Catalyst publication *Mentoring: A Guide to Corporate Programs and Practices*. Catalyst reported that in 1990 the Association of Management Women's Westchester chapter at NYNEX initiated innovative "mentoring circles . . . to address members' career development and planning needs." The circles, most of which were composed exclusively of women, facilitated "interaction between the different levels of the organization and provide[d] greater opportunities to develop relationships." While the participants were not always equal in terms of talents, experience, or level, when the women sat down together to share experience and learn from one another, they were equal. Catalyst quoted Rosemary Gift, a member of the implementation committee, in summarizing what makes the circles work. "Groups that truly work," Gift said, "are those in which the mentors and mentees are willing to risk being open and vulnerable."

As is often the case with mentoring in today's workplace, getting promoted to the next-level job is not a mentoring group goal. Instead, women are exposed to a range of perspectives on business-related issues, including work-family balance and life satisfaction. Mary, a mid-level manager I spoke with in New York, had participated in a company-sponsored mentoring group. "The value of a mentoring circle," Mary told me, "is not to get people promoted.

For me, the value came from meeting other women from very different areas in our large company and learning from others how I could do what I do better. I haven't been promoted, but knowing where my job fits in the big picture has led me to better enjoy my job, and probably to do it better as well."

Amy Burgess, president of WOW'M: The Mentoring Company in Denver, sees Mentoring Circles™ as offering the best of male- and female-style mentoring: male mentoring that focuses on action and leads to relationship, and female mentoring that begins with relationship and leads to action. "When Mentoring Circles become infused with trust and commitment," Amy says from experience, "the members move from frustration to possibility." "The purpose of Mentoring Circles," Amy goes on to say, "is to develop self-efficacy and leadership. Mentoring is about transferring knowledge, insight, and experience. The process that happens in Mentoring Circles leads individuals to discover and learn."

Amy has worked with Coors Brewing Company, Hewlett-Packard, and the Institute for Women and Leadership at Colorado State University to implement Mentoring Circles for women leaders. "The purpose of the Mentoring Circles at Colorado State," Dr. Elnora Gilfoyle, director of the institute and former provost for the university, told me, "is to provide a process by which university culture could become a more 'just place' for women."

What goes on in Mentoring Circles is mentoring because, as Ellie said, "the participants share real life experiences and ask for the help they want." Each circle consists of ten people plus a primary mentor and a facilitator who does not participate herself but keeps the discussions focused and on track. Each woman brings a current challenge she is facing, for example, "Should I go for the promotion?" The group discusses the challenge and how different scenarios might affect the group member. As the woman receives mentoring from the resource group, the other members and the primary mentor learn about the system, or workplace, of which they are all a part. Ellie was primary mentor for a Personnel Group made up of state-classified women, administrative professionals, and faculty members. She shared with the group her experiences as provost and her interest in being department head in Occupational Therapy. The group offered their experiences, observations, and support as Ellie let the circle mentor her through her challenge.

Ellie believes that Mentoring Circles respect female culture more than any other career growth and development process. "We do not give advice," she makes clear. "Advice puts one in a power relationship. Advice is threatening. Within the circle, members share stories and assimilate another's experience." "We came in [to the circle] with global issues hanging over us," said a woman from the Personnel Circle. "Through facilitation, we were able to focus on specific issues and accomplish specific goals."

The Mentoring Circles at Colorado State University function to validate participants' strengths and competencies. Women gained the "courage to act on their values, to assume leadership roles, to create change, and to celebrate their victories."

Imagine the mentoring power that a group of women can bring. Based on a commitment to communication and a foundation of trust, women can bring their quests and their questions to the group and receive information, insights, suggestions, and support from an exciting range of perspectives.

Mentoring groups represent a developmental and growth process that is wonderfully adaptable to women's needs and goals.

If your company or workplace has a mentoring group or groups, find out how you can participate. If no such opportunity exists, you can be the initiator. The effort will reward you many times over, and the potential benefits for all the women who will share and learn are endless.

Weekend Mentoring

The concept of group mentoring has caught on beyond corporate walls. Across the country, women are coming together to participate in mentoring experiences for one day, one weekend, or a sequence of weekends. Amy Burgess, psychotherapist and president of WOW'M, the Mentoring Company, had the idea for the WOW'M mentoring events a few years ago. Amy's commitment to women learning from women has brought many wonderful women together as participants and mentors in one- and two-day sessions that have featured such speakers as Anita Rodick, founder of The Body Shop. Women who are accomplished in their careers, professions, and creative activities come to the workshops prepared to share what they know with the protégés who sign up for the learning experience. The weekend I participated as a mentor, I was joined by Caroline Turner, then chief legal officer for Coors Brewing Company and now a senior vice president.

Through guided activities, the protégés at WOW'M events select women with whom they want to learn. In small groups led by an invited member, we talk about our career plans, our challenges, and our life dreams. The WOW'M Mentoring Circles celebrate women's way of being and the rich learning we can offer one another through caring and sharing our experiences and our stories. Women leave these mentoring workshops energized about their careers and dreams, and reaffirmed as capable and potential whole people. If you would be interested in creating a mentoring day or weekend for women seeking the wisdom of women, contact Amy Burgess at WOW'M in Denver for her help and direction.

Coaches for Hire

You are a high-potential woman, and your company wants to make sure you stay. There are no official programs at your corporation to match you with an experienced and influential mentor within the system. You are good, and you may be poised to be the woman who first breaks your company's glass ceiling. What you need, the top executives at your workplace decide, is a coach who will polish your rough edges, train you in organizational savvy, and feed you the information you need if you are to achieve and hold a top position. Where do they go to find this coach/mentor to guide your career ascent? A number of Fortune 500 companies are going to the outside, to coaches for hire, to prepare their high-potential women for a future above the glass ceiling.

"I work as a private coach/consultant for men and women," an experienced corporate coach told me.

I do not consider myself a mentor because for me to be a mentor is something magic that comes from the heart. I am a coach because I know how to play the game. Plenty of women who have succeeded and broken the glass ceiling don't always know the process they went through. They may not make good mentors for those who follow because they can't trace where they've been. I study the organization and know the process someone must follow if she's to break through.

This woman emphasizes that confidentiality is sacred in her profession and will not discuss profiles of her past or current clients. Before becoming a coach/consultant, she worked in areas where knowing how to play the game was what made her a success. Now she sells her knowhow to corporations that hire her to coach their high-potential women. "Yes," she said, "my clients are corporations; the people I work with are mostly the women they want to promote, the high flyers they need to retrain."

"J" works with her assigned protégés for as long as the company believes she is making a difference and producing results. "These arrangements aren't marriages based on affection," "J" emphasized. "They are business connections designed to help a person develop her full potential as a manager. I study the organization, we do assessments, I coach her on skills she needs, and I give feedback on her performance." And, "J" assured me, her clients get top value for their dollar.

Your company may not be in a position to hire a coach for you, but you can hire one for yourself.

Another option you have if you are having difficulty
finding a mentor, a mentoring group, or a satisfac-
tory peer mentoring relationship is to hire someone
to serve as your counselor, your confident, your
coach, and/or your business adviser!

Consultants for hire come in a variety of categories, from very focused business coaches, to career/life coaches, to social workers
and counselors on call who act as confidants for women under stress
as a result of their career and workplace demands.

According to an article on corporate coaching by Sharon L.
Peters that appeared in *USA Today* on May 10, 1996, the "hire-a-
confidant phenomenon is almost exclusively a female thing." The
women who call for counseling and coaching are healthy, productive women who need to talk to someone who understands the many
facets of women's experience. With a phone call they can connect
with someone who appreciates the "emotionality factor in making
unpleasant personnel decisions to coming to terms with competition
with other women," said Joyce Jordan, a Raleigh, N.C., clinical
social worker who serves as counselor-on-call for several female
clients.

Many women need to talk through stressful times and difficult
decisions. The talk helps them bring a complex of factors into the
foreground and organize a response.

As many women business owners and top executives know,
finding a mentor we can trust with our vulnerabilities and questions—someone who will always have time for us—can be extremely difficult. When they need to talk and there is no one in the
next office to listen, more and more women are calling on the resources of trained and knowledgeable business coaches. "Unlike
therapists or counselors, business coaches offer specific business
advice," wrote Peters.

In the same article from *USA Today*, Lori Pedelty, head of
Capstone Consulting in Chicago and a business coach has reported
that her clients have talked about how to smooth out rough relation-

ships with employees, demoting employees, after a promotion, due to nonperformance, and being a more effective leader and communicator.

Janet Duvall, a former county commissioner and now a coach in Colorado, works with women "seeking wholeness; women who want their lives to be more." She sees her role as being "someone in your corner; someone to help you take the next step." Janet's purpose as a coach is to help a woman be who she is."Coaching is a professional relationship," Janet makes clear. "It is not a friendship, and it is not favor." Coaching can cost from $60 to $200 an hour, and there are institutes and colleges that provide training and certification for the coaches.

Micki McMillan is an organizational consultant and certified business coach. Before starting her own business, she was the highest-ranking woman in operations at a public service company, managing a $20 million budget and having more than 300 employees reporting to her. When Micki's mentor came to feel threatened by Micki's success, that mentor was no longer available as a "friend, resource, and sounding board." Like many other high ranking females, Micki missed the interaction with her mentor. Many women learn through talk and appreciate the validation that comes from being understood. "Today, as a coach," Micki said, "I can help a person get in touch with her own sense of power. I do not recommend solutions. I do help identify deficits and reflect back suggestions that help people guide their own solutions. I coach people to get in touch with where they are and help them create a future. I can help women change how they live their lives. When I am coaching," Micki concluded, "my soul just sings."

Business coaches I have spoken with want to emphasize that coaching is not therapy. Coaches do not work on "issues" or delve much into the past. Coaches work in the present and for the future. They help you set the personal and professional goals that will give you the life you really want.

The trend to coaches for hire meets the needs of women today. Women who have become coaches can help women through the difficult life choices we face. "Most women," says Lori Pedelty of

Capstone Consulting, "have a stronger need than men to see a career as something that contributes to their happiness and fulfillment." You can find these coaches and use them to listen, to function as mirrors, and to contribute to the growth and development you seek for yourself as a fulfilled woman.

Some women who are reluctant to approach a volunteer mentor and ask her for her commitment, attention, and support are more comfortable when they can pay for the services they believe will help them in their careers. This way, Paula explained in a confidential conversation, "I don't feel personally obligated. I would feel wretched if I took my mentor's time and disappointed her. This way [hiring a coach/mentor] I am exchanging money for the coaching, the information, and the guidance. I feel better about it that way."

Hiring a coach/mentor can help you take an objective look at yourself, assess your assets and your weaknesses, and get the coaching you need in order to develop your strengths and achieve a successful and fulfilling life. Having trained coaches who are available to work with you and support your growth gives you a marvelous advantage. You can specify the type of coaching/mentoring you want and the type of person with whom you will be most comfortable. The coaches I have met with convince me that their goal is for you to always be your authentic self and to develop where your powers and values lead. For many women, part of being who we are, our strength, is our willingness to reach out and learn from the wisdom and guidance of others. Coaches for hire give everyone this opportunity—and this benefit.

If You Want to Learn More

The Internet is an excellent way to learn about coaching and to be connected with a coach who is appropriate for your needs and goals. You can contact Coach University at *www.coach.com* for information about the coaching concept and how you can become involved.

You can also find mentors on line. You can e-mentor without

leaving your office or home. Via the Internet, you can have the benefits of a committed learning relationship with a knowledgeable mentor who will respect confidentiality and give you the information and support you want.

Here are just a few of the many sites you can visit and learn more:

The Woman to Woman Mentoring Program "matches women with experience in business, the Internet, computers, and other areas to provide the best in learning experience for those who apply for a mentor." (www.womensresourcentr.org/mentor/mentorap)

Electra Mentoring Connection "Electra and *womenCONNECT. com* have joined together in creating ELECTRA's MENTORING CONNECTION where women beginning or changing their careers (protégés) can find experienced professional women (mentors) to guide them." (mentor.electra.com/electra)

"MentorNet," the National Electronic Industrial Mentoring Network for Women in Engineering and Science. (www.advancing-women.com/wk_mentornet.html)

Menttium 100, an innovative project "designed to help fast-track women to hook up with mentors outside their own companies" (*Fortune*, February 1, 1999). Also of interest is Menttium's sister company and cross-company program for professionals of color. (www.menttium.com)

CHAPTER 9

Extending the Wisdom

YOU ARE IN a place today that many women before you would envy. Women who have gone before you have knowledge and experience to share with you in an exchange of gifts for our future. You know who you want to be and what you want to achieve. You have the expectations that will become your future, and women with insight and wisdom will help to guide you toward realizing the goal.

You may have found a mentor to participate with you in your growth and development process. Or perhaps you have established a mentoring connection with your peers at work or with a coach or mentor you have found through local resources or over the Internet. Whether formal or informal, these relationships involve trust, commitment, and the time to know each other and be known. Your goals may be formal and broken down into measurable objectives and deliverables, or informal and encouraged by spontaneous opportunity, intuitive guidance, and honest feedback. Whether formal or informal, one-on-one or with peers or within mentoring groups, mentoring means connecting with women who will be a resource for your career and life development.

Coming together with women and benefiting from learning and giving is not limited to the circumstances that we have labeled mentoring. Networking, ethnic circles, friends with a focus, affinity groups, and defined action groups can all evolve into mentoring opportunities. In fact, often much of what goes on in these settings is mentoring. When women come together for the purpose of connecting as women and sharing who they are with one another, we create an opportunity to discover ourselves and who we can become.

139

Networks

Today's networks are different from the make-a-contact, get-a-job networks of the past, where women were instructed to "never talk about children, husbands, pets, or recipes" and "never share anything personal about your struggles and concerns." Today, women's networks of all descriptions and degrees of formality are creating opportunities for women to come together and learn from one another. They offer places where women can discuss their careers and their professions, and also talk about being a woman whose life encompasses a multiplicity of facets and functions. Women are drawn to these groups at work and in their communities. From Virginia to Oregon, women are meeting in forums and action groups to become stronger together.

You may have a magnificent mentor or a group of mentors, and that's an advantage for you. You also can benefit, however, from attending or joining a network in which you feel comfortable, to which you are willing to contribute, and from which you can continue your learning.

Corporate Networks and Forums

"Today, corporate women's groups are enjoying a new credibility as business-minded entities that work for—rather than against—company goals," reported Catalyst, the New York–based research organization. "Indeed progressive companies recognize that corporate women's groups are a low-cost way to enhance communication, identify 'glass ceiling' issues, test pilot coaching and mentoring programs, boost employee morale as well as company image, and develop the leadership skills of members." Fifty-one percent of women's networks surveyed by Catalyst received company funds, according to *Creating Women's Networks: A How to Guide for Women & Companies*, Jossey Bass, 1999.

According to Catalyst, over half of these women's groups advise management on women's concerns; 49 percent were initiated by senior women; 88 percent are allowed to use company facilities and resources; and 45 percent have a designated management liaison.

I visited with Holly Walkland, first chairperson of the Kodak Women's Forum, and with Jody Dietz, human resources development strategist, at their Rochester, New York, facility. At the time I visited, the Women's Forum of Kodak Employees was the largest women's corporate network in the United States, with a membership of over 500. Holly and Jody, proud of what their forum has accomplished for women, pointed to improved opportunities to take on project management and other leadership responsibilities that give them experience and visibility. "It is very easy for women to develop in this supportive environment," Holly and Jody told me.

Kodak has six forums at its national headquarters, including a Veterans Network of Kodak Employees, a Native American Council, an African-American network, HOLA (Hispanic Organization for Leadership in America), and Lamba, an organization to respond to the needs of gay, lesbian, and bisexual employees and their allies at Kodak. And Kodak is only one of many corporations that sponsor such forums and networks. Dr. Joan Lester, author of *Taking Charge: Every Woman's Action Guide to Personal, Political & Professional Success* and founder of the Equity Institute in California, finds it encouraging that more corporations than ever before are sponsoring these groups. She believes that in many business settings, 90 to 95 percent of gays and lesbians are not out, but that the existence of these new gay and lesbian networks will send a message to those in the closet that to identify oneself as gay or lesbian is accepted within the corporate environment.

Women's networks give women exposure to new responsibilities. In addition, the mission of many networks is to provide women with a forum for addressing issues that affect women in the workplace and to present seminars and speakers that offer members new skills and ideas.

141

One rainy Valentine's Day I was the invited speaker for the first meeting of the Bechtel Women's Initiative (BWI) forum in San Francisco. Close to sixty women and six or seven men attended the session. I was impressed with the group's organization and focus, and I asked to have a copy of its mission statement as an example of how a corporate women's group defines itself.

The BWI mission statement reads as follows:

The Bechtel Women's Initiative (BWI) provides a forum for addressing the issues that are unique to women employees of Bechtel, with the purpose of enhancing their ability to support the company's business objectives and promote Bechtel as the employer of choice. The objectives of BWI are to:

Share issues and experiences and explore topics of mutual interest;

Educate and develop skills to enhance each employee's ability to contribute to the company as well as facilitate career development;

Provide counsel, suggestions and input to management on key issues and act as a change agent in support of the company's diversity initiatives, particularly for women in the workplace.

Not only will you benefit from the learning opportunities within these networks, but many women's forums give mid-level and entry-level women opportunities to meet and interact with upper-level women outside of the workplace hierarchy. "I got my job because of our women's network," a manager at Corning International told me. Karen is a member of the Women's Forum, an organization at Corning that runs events and promotes women meeting women. "I was being considered for a new assignment with my current group," Karen explained.

This was good, but I was actually interested in another group in another division. At a forum meeting, I bumped into a woman from the other division. I asked her if any-thing was coming up in her area. She said "Yes, I just might have something." It turned out that she did, and it was because of the network, where all women feel com-fortable being together, that I could approach her com-fortably about a position.

Karen ended her story by saying that she would not have felt right barging in and contacting this woman by phone. In person, though, she had felt that talking with her was okay.

Today more senior women than ever before are becoming in-volved with and starting groups and networks with junior women. In years past, these same senior women had chosen to assimilate and identify with their male colleagues. Now these upper-level women are becoming more willing to be part of a network encourag-ing women to seek advancement in corporate environments. Some of these busy women do not have time to mentor a protégé, but by attending networking sessions and forum meetings, they make themselves available to junior women and add authority and value to the networking activity.

For women seeking a mentor, joining a network does not mean that you have abandoned one option for a female learning connec-tion in favor of another. Women looking for mentors may be able to spark mentoring connections through contact at a network with sen-ior women they might never have met or talked with before. Often from women's forums comes the impetus to develop mentoring pro-grams for women in the division or the corporation.

One such program at a Hewlett-Packard division in Colorado, Women's Information Network (WIN), recently celebrated the suc-cessful conclusion of its first formal matched-mentors program. Ac-cording to an engineer with Hewlett-Packard and one of the project's developers, WIN plans to begin the selection and match-ing process again for a new group of protégés.

It is important, from a corporate perspective, that these spon-sored networks and forums provide more than just interaction op-portunities for women. They must provide tangible results in terms of women's productivity and job satisfaction if they are to continue. "If these networks fail," I learned during my conversation with Tara Levine at Catalyst, "it will be because they have had too little structure, because too much emphasis has been put on consensus, or because they have been too action-oriented without enough attention to learning from and with each other. Women can't be viewed as just getting together to talk," said one catalyst member. "They need concrete results to show those who scrutinize that there has been solid value in the activity."

Discover if a network exists where you work. If one does, attend a session and determine if making connection with the women involved would benefit you. If your corporation or workplace does not have a network, contact Catalyst in New York for its most recent information on establishing and maintaining women's networks. Also, give yourself a break and don't feel you have to reinvent the wheel. Find out what other companies have networks and what they will share with you about these networks' mission and structure. Chances are you will be inundated with information and will meet some interesting women in the process.

Going Beyond the Corporate Boundaries

When corporate forums do not exist, and even when they do, women also can look outside their immediate business or employer to find networks and women's groups to join. One group of powerful women did just this more than ten years ago, and their network continues to operate.

The idea came in 1982 from a committee of the National Organization of Business Women. Rosabeth Moss Kanter conducted the first search. To be selected as a member of this premier group of businesswomen, a woman had to be president or CEO of a $10 million privately held company or a $50 million public company. Two of the original members were Christy Heffner of *Playboy* magazine and Ellen Gordon of Tootsie Roll. The group is called the Committee of 200. The idea was to bring these women together for networking, so that they could get to know one another and learn from one another's experiences. Most of the women in this elite network work with men, so one of the pleasures of coming together is that they can talk about their experiences as women—and learn from one another!

"We get together twice a year," Kathryn Hach, chair of Hach Company and an original Committee of 200 member, told me. "Nobody is shy. We have formal speakers and hold an informal conference." What Kitty Hach enjoys most about the network gatherings is that "When we get together, we talk. We talk like a house on fire!"

As I was just beginning this book, I was invited to attend and "listen in" on a national meeting of AWSCPA (American Women's Society of CPAs). I asked a member of the board of directors of this group, why, when there were other professional organizations for public accountants, she found membership in an all-female group to be valuable and worth her time and effort. "Because there is advantage to being with your own kind," she answered. "There's a mutual sharing, understanding, and caring that can come only from other women who share our backgrounds and experiences."

She went on to say that it had been difficult to get money from the "big six" accounting firms and to stay afloat as an all-women's group, but that the struggle has been worth it. "Being an all-women's group gives our female members an opportunity to take on responsibilities and get some recognition that might not happen in a large organization," she explained. "It's a learning and a growing experience for us, not just a chance to come together and do a reality check."

Yet the need for a reality check is exactly what motivates some women to join women's professional organizations. "I work with men all day," Diana, a water resources engineer, told me. "I need to come together with other women engineers and scientists to see if what I'm perceiving tracks with their reality—and to find out from them what they are doing to keep themselves sane!" Diana has found such a group of women to interact with through a chapter of the Society of Women in Science and Engineering in the city where she works.

Other women's network groups go beyond both corporate and professional walls to bring women together in environments for sharing and learning. These networks exist in towns and cities all over the country. One such network in Fort Collins, Colorado, has recently celebrated its twentieth anniversary! Nancy Valentine, new to town as a management recruiter in 1970, found herself building rapport with women in human resources positions. Nancy suggested that they meet for lunch and that each bring another friend or associate. Today more than one hundred women from independent businesses, the professions, and corporations meet once a month for lunch at a local hotel. The program includes speakers and an opportunity for women to introduce themselves and their businesses to one another. Dues cover a newsletter with feature articles contributed by the members. "The network," Nancy says with pride and appreciation, "is my mentor."

Joining established women's professional groups can be a fine way to expand your personal resource network and learn with other women what is happening for women in your business or profession and how to make the most effective moves toward success. I have spoken with women in real estate, women insurance agents, nursing organizations, women trial lawyers, the Alliance of Business and Professional Women, the American Association of Business Women, a network of women in higher education in southern Ohio, women's chambers of commerce, an organization for federally employed women, and many other women's groups and organizations that exist outside the corporate walls. The programs these groups sponsor, including mentoring programs, offer excellent learning opportunities for women of all ages at all stages in their careers.

Ethnic Groups and Networks

If you are a women of color in today's workplace, you may well feel alone or isolated from the mainstream of women and men in your organization. Catalyst, the New York–based organization promoting women in executive positions, tells us that of the 57.8 million women in the workforce, 23 percent are minorities. However, women of color make up only 14 percent of the 2.9 million women in managerial positions. For a woman of color, finding a mentor can be challenging for a number of reasons. There are a limited number of women of color in the managerial ranks who are available to junior women. And when a woman does find someone of her own race or ethnicity that she wants as a mentor, Ann Kusumoto, a management consultant in the Los Angeles area, said in an article by Tamina Davar for *Careers and the Woman MBA*, published by Crimson & Brown Associates, the pair can face "resentment from white colleagues who may perceive the relationship as 'exclusionary' rather than supportive and affirming."

A woman of color also has to assess her potential mentor's attitudes concerning cultural adaptation and assimilation before committing herself to a public, visible protégé/mentor relationship.

Once a mentoring relationship is established, however, the connection can provide valuable information and guidance for you as the protégé, and give your mentor an opportunity to introduce another woman into a position of influence where, together, neither of you will be alone.

You may not be fortunate enough to connect with a mentor of your background or ethnicity at the place where you work. You can, though, reach out to join with other women in groups formed around ethnicity and/or race. Coming together and sharing your goals and experiences, your wisdom and encouragement, in these groups can be extremely important to your affirmation of self and to your satisfaction in your work situation. Women of color need one another, not only to advance one another's careers, but for emotional and relationship support as well.

"Often for African American women working in a predominantly white workplace culture, there is no contact with other African American women," Lusandra, an elementary school teacher with plans to become a principal, told me. "Our group is a place I can come and just be me. It's a group where I'm not the only one with big hips!" For Brenda, a manager for a large Denver area employer, this is a group where other women "walk her walk."

Nicole, an African American woman and experienced management consultant invited me to attend a Saturday session of her African American women's mentoring group. This particular group represents a broad spectrum of careers and professions. Its members come together to experience a "wholeness and spirituality that the sisters recognize in each other."

"African American women are bicultural," Nicole explained. "The members of this group are American by nature and African American by nurture. We come together as a group to acknowledge and protect the 'inner me,' the self voice inside that tells me what I need to be about."

"We are a spiritual group," Sylvia added. "When we talk about being spiritual, we are not being subversive, as non-African Americans in our workplaces might think. Spirituality to us is not religiosity; it simply means that there are beings who are greater than we. As a group we understand that together, and it gives us something back."

The women in this organization come together to encourage and learn from one another in a way that is consistent with their history. "African American women have been separated from their history," said Anita, a self-employed woman in the nonprofit sector. "In our tradition, each one would teach what she knows. Elder women were the mentors. They gave what they knew. Their degrees come from living, not from schooling."

When they come together, it is to share with one another what they know, and to grow in a place where they can be themselves.

Many such groups for women of particular races or ethnicities exist, and more are forming. They give women of non-Eurocentric backgrounds places to come together and learn from one another how to succeed in their bicultural lives and careers.

For six Latina women at a high-tech corporation in the West, coming together informally every six weeks has provided them with a place to be authentic and a place to ask questions and learn from one another how to move ahead in their jobs and their lives. "We never mention the word *mentoring*," Josie told me.

> But that's what we're doing. We're social, that's the norm for us. We're more comfortable giving than asking, but being in a group makes asking easier. Someone may wonder how she fits into the organization, and we all try to give her our stories and our ideas. Women also ask questions for the group, like "Should I move or not?" or "I've tried this, but it's not working. Why?" We talk strategy, we talk about our children and our lives. We laugh and sometimes we cry. We come together to be ourselves and to learn from and support one another. People at the next table may think we are just a bunch of Latina women getting together to have a good time. We are having a good time, but we're also providing a home for one another. We're mentoring together, growing together, and feeling good about ourselves in the process.

You can be the initiator. Invite women like yourself to come together informally to talk and share and teach and learn. Perhaps finding a place to be authentic, to be known and affirmed, will be what you need to enhance your life and add to your work and life satisfaction. However, if you see potential for the group to take on a more formal agenda, perhaps to initiate a mentoring program for minority women within your organization, go ahead. Learning and growing often means taking action. Learning, growing, and taking action together will give us a better tomorrow.

Action Groups and Power Groups

Your growth and development will be enhanced when you can find a place that affirms and encourages who you are and what you want to achieve. Today women who want to take charge of their lives are creating action groups to support one another in achieving personal growth and reaching career goals.

In her book *Taking Charge,* Joan Lester ended each of her milestone chapters with a suggested agenda for an action group. The action groups she identified bring women together to help one another reach milestones in their personal, professional, and political lives. Action groups can be fairly formal, with agreed-upon agendas and evaluations of how you are progressing toward achieving your goals. They also can be more free-form, with women coming together on a regular basis to ask for ideas and help in confronting their more immediate challenges.

One exciting example of a focused action group is the A Team, a group of Boston-area women who came together in 1984 and vowed to help and motivate one another toward landing top jobs in the health-care profession. "The women were tied together only by their gender, a common profession, and a desire to share information and advice," according to a *New York Times* article by Andrea Gabor. The group set a firm goal: "To establish at least three of its members in executive suites within a few years."

To achieve their goals, the members of the A Team—through a highly methodical process—used phones, head hunters, local politicians, and even conducted seminars. "Working together with a one-for-all attitude, these women succeeded beyond what they had imagined," writes Gabor.

Power groups follow the concept of action groups; they bring women together not with the primary purpose of discovering and becoming together but as a base for accomplishing an established political agenda. Naomi Wolf in *Fire With Fire* envisioned these groups as "a new form of social organization." If the term *power group* feels too threatening, Wolf suggested *resource group* as an alternative term. She called attention to the fact that "Affiliation groups have a long history for women; the world of white women's clubs fostered the actions that won women the vote, and African-American women's clubs were active in fighting lynching." She went on to argue that the resource group provides a comfortable community as well as developing a "new psychology of power and consolidating female clout."

Children of the West is a group of bright, informed women in Wyoming, Colorado, and Virginia who drive hundreds of miles to come together as a power group committed to creating forums for harmony among western land interests. They formed as a group to develop literature and lobby congressmen and senators in Washington, D.C., for ranching rights. They are affiliated with other groups and organizations, but they formed Children of the West purposely as a women's group to rally women's commitment, strengths, and sense of values in promoting their convictions. During our first session in Rock Springs, Wyoming, I asked the women, who at that point were searching for a mission and direction after the lobbying activity had ended, what value they saw for themselves in continuing Children of the West. Jean Dickinson, one of the ranching women from Wyoming/Colorado, said that one of the most important reasons she wanted to continue coming together as a group was "because of the mentoring I get from being with these women whose values and style I respect." Carol and Penny agreed that being women together was an opportunity for learning from the group's pooled experience. Children of the West is preparing itself to become a player in resolving western land conflicts by offering scholarships, participating on state committees, and staying involved with educational opportunities for young people interested in a ranching career.

Affinity Groups That Enhance Our Experience as Women

Linda Fairstein, chief of the Sex Crimes Prosecution Unit of the New York County District Attorney's office and author of *Sexual Violence,* and a series of crime novels, meets monthly with a group of highly successful, influential women like herself. Some of the faces, she told me, anyone would recognize: They belong to prominent women in the media, and we see them every day. Others we might not recognize: These women hold high-level positions in banking, business, and the professions. Linda respectfully declined to name the women who refer to themselves as "members" of this group.

The members do not think of what they are doing as networking, a word Linda hates. Rather, Linda and her friends see themselves as a semiformalized affinity group coming together to offer one another support and community. Everyone who attends has been invited to join by another woman already in the group. Sometimes they talk about their work, sometimes about politics, sometimes about being prominent women with extremely demanding schedules. Often they laugh. Some have become close personal friends, others look forward to joining the group for lunch but have not formed intimate friendships. Scheduling time together at the round table in the restaurant window has become a priority in their busy lives. They welcome this place where they can be themselves, where they can retreat from their public positions to become part of a community of women who share their strength and offer their wisdom as they give to and receive from one another.

All over the country, from Florida to Oregon, women are coming together in restaurants, in living rooms, in conference centers, and even on outdoor adventures to form giving and learning communities. Sometimes an issue brings women together to accomplish a community action goal. Often, though, women are drawn to one another for the strength that comes from being ourselves together. As women, we can share the way we learn through the telling of the stories of our lives and by listening to one another's stories. Then we can offer counsel and guidance that considers our wholeness and the quality of the life we want to accomplish along with the titles and salaries we want to achieve.

Fortune magazine in September 1995 presented an article by Betsy Morris entitled "Executive Women Confront Midlife Crisis." The banner read: "It is a time of reckoning for the first big generation of women to hit the age of 40 in a business suit. But for many career women, even talking about it carries a whiff of betrayal." How do women confront their crises, and how do they gain understanding of themselves so that they can make the right decisions for their lives? One way, suggested by this article, is that they come together to listen to and counsel one another. They form a group around a life crisis they need to confront, where they can find support through other women whose thinking and perspective they seek. As Morris reported:

> Shoya Zichy's pale-yellow living room on the Upper East Side has become an unlikely refuge for some of the best and brightest career women in New York City. In the past year they have made the pilgrimage here, sometimes in groups, sometimes alone, to visit with Ms. Zinchy—to sip her wine, take in her oil paintings, seek her counsel, or counsel each other. Here they share their darkest secrets; they can be outrageously un-PC; they don't have to make any apologies."

And who are these women seeking counsel and other women to provide that counsel?

> They are serious career women. They are trailblazers. They think lateral moves are for losers. But increasingly they have become unhappy with their lives, and some of them have made big changes.

Women are forming groups around age and stage, single-parent issues, advocacy for older parents, lifestyle values, spiritual searches, and career shifts. We learn from one another and we give to one another. We approach life as a whole, knowing the interconnectedness of all our decisions. We seek one another's wisdom as we continue composing our lives.

You have the opportunity to begin now to form your groups and share in the wisdom. Don't wait. Reach out and invite women you know to learn and grow together. Your friendship groups, like your groups at work or in your profession, can be so much more than venues for venting.

When you ask women for help in managing your
work challenge and your life balance issues, you are
going beyond venting to inventing.

And, with the resource of other women, you will invent the solutions
that will bring satisfaction to your career and your life. With your
friends, your sisters, your colleagues, you can find the collaborative
mentoring you need to become the person you want to be.

Twenty-five years ago I belonged to a book group that brought
nine women together, ostensibly to talk about books, but more im-
portantly to share with one another the frustrations and joys of our
lives—to raise our consciousness about being women. Eventually
we left our children at elementary schools and reentered our professions. We still meet, though, and share with one another the stories
of our lives. I wish now that I had asked more directly for mentoring
from these women rather than hoping in our friendly exchanges to
catch a clue here and there for understanding my life and guiding
my growth. Instead of being indirect and telling stories from my
present circumstances, I wish I had asked, "Can you help me know
if I should return to teaching or begin a business?" Or, "What do
you know about committing to a new business and staying involved
in the lives of three young children? How much can I take on, and
what will have the most meaning and the best results?"

I know now that they were waiting to be asked, just as I waited
to be asked by them for my insights, my experiences, and what I
had of a woman's wisdom. Don't hesitate and miss the opportunity
to learn. Ask, and be willing to give in return. The riches will multi-
ply. We will all become wiser, and our collected wisdom will have
power to change the world.

Our Future Learning Together

Our mentors, our networks, our professional groups, our action
groups, our power groups, and our affinity groups bring us together

to benefit from the essential connections we share with other women.

Your mentors can be the gateway to your future and to the future for women in the workplace. When you make the mentoring connection with another woman, you are reaching out for her wisdom and for her guidance. You are putting yourself in a position to learn from a woman about a woman's experience. She has lived the challenges and rewards of being a woman with a career, earning recognition for her talents and her performance.

Though her choices concerning work/family/community may not be what you will choose, chances are that she has faced the dilemmas you will face and can offer you her stories and her insights. She is your history text and your wise counselor. Together you will construct the issues and frame the solutions that will change the workplace for women and for the future of all people who want to live productive and fulfilled lives.

Back in the 1970s, as women committed to a lifetime in the workplace, we were encouraged to assimilate, to become like the men who had designed the system and who held the power. Today women tell me that they don't want to assimilate, to give up who they are to fit into a system they didn't create. They see women who have proven their worth through their intelligence, skills, talents, and leadership style holding high-level positions and taking charge. Many have struggled to achieve their rewards, and some have sacrificed dimensions of themselves in the process.

Each generation, each wave, each year brings new women into the workforce with questions about how to approach their careers and their personal growth. The female style of mentoring brings women together in a mutual learning connection. Together you and your mentor approach your developmental needs and life decisions. Your women mentors have the wisdom of their experience. They will give you support and direction in understanding your options; they will not, in most cases, give you direct advice that they expect you to follow verbatim. Rather, women present themselves in mentoring relationships as ready to explore, to share, and to learn together. Women recognize one another. As different as we are in personality and background, we share the experience of being female. With your woman mentor or mentors you can be genuinely yourself, reaching out to the wisdom of women in the process of becoming yourself.

You must take the initiative, asking for the gifts and offering your gifts in return. Women have always learned from other women, but we haven't learned as much as women have to offer. We observed our mothers, our teachers, and women ahead of us in their careers and professions. We talked and talked with our friends and with our sisters, but did we make it clear that we respected their wisdom and really wanted to hear their stories and learn from their experience? Some of us were too busy proving our independence to admit that we didn't have all the answers, or even all the questions. Others of us didn't want to seem a burden or to bind another women in a tangle of obligation.

Today you have much to offer in the gift exchange. You have your perspective, your experience, your questions, and your willingness to stretch for solutions. You don't have to wait to be asked. Women are waiting to be included in a learning opportunity. Ask to become part of the gift exchange with another woman as your mentor. Become a mentor yourself. Bring groups of women together to learn from one another and to build a future where we can be ourselves and be strong in our authenticity. I think often of Susan Skogg, author of *Embracing Our Essence*, when I imagine women in mentoring groups. "Women find strength and benefit in community," she told me as we had lunch together recently. "We find a lushness of spirit when coming together with other women."

It is in this lushness of spirit that women will mentor and grow together. As we become involved in mutual development and growth, we will become vested in one another's futures. When we give and when we receive, we form a bond that unites us in accomplishing our goals and our dreams. Together we will contribute to a healthy tomorrow for women, and to a workplace that honors whole people living fulfilled and satisfying lives.

If You Want to Learn More

Catalyst. *Creating Women's Networks: A How-To Guide for Women and Companies* (New York: Catalyst, 1999).

DiMona, Lisa, and Constance Herndon, editors. *The 1995 Women's Sourcebook* (Boston: Houghton Mifflin, 1994).

Hadley, Joyce, and Betsy Sheldon. *The Smart Woman's Guide to Networking* (Franklin Lakes, N.J.: Career Press, 1995).

Lester, Joan Steinau. *Taking Charge: Every Woman's Guide to Personal, Political & Professional Success* (Berkeley, Calif.: Conari Press, 1996).

Rosoff, Ilene, editor. *The Woman Source Catalog & Review: Tools for Connecting the Community of Women*, updated revised edition (Berkeley, Calif.: Celestial Arts, 1997).

Bibliography

"Are You Entering the Same Male-Dominated Work Force as Your Predecessors?" *Graduate Engineering*, February 1994.

Autry, James A. *Love and Profit: The Art of Caring Leadership* (New York: Avon Books, 1991).

Barrentine, Pat, ed. *When the Canary Stops Singing: Women's Perspective on Transforming Business* (San Francisco: Berrett-Koehler, 1993).

Bateson, Mary Catherine. *Composing a Life* (New York: Plume, 1990).

Blom, Eric. "For Women, a Woman's Hand." *(Portland) Maine Sunday Telegram*, April 15, 1990.

Blum, Deborah. *Sex On the Brain: Biologial Differences Between Men and Women* (New York: Viking, 1997).

Briles, Judith. *The Briles Report on Women in Healthcare: Changing Conflict to Collaboration in a Toxic Workplace* (San Francisco: Jossey-Bass, 1994).

Bylsma, Wayne H., and others. "Comparing Gender Differences in Entitlement at Work and in Relationships." Paper presented at the Annual Meeting of the Eastern Psychological Association, Buffalo, N.Y., April 21–24, 1988.

Byrne, John. "Let a Mentor Lead You." *Business Week*, April 20, 1987, p. 95.

Cantor, Dorothy W., and Toni Bernay with Jean Stoess. *Women in Power: The Secrets of Leadership* (Boston: Houghton Mifflin, 1992).

Carr-Ruffino, Norma. *The Promotable Woman: Becoming a Successful Manager*, rev. ed. (Belmont, Calif.: Wadsworth Publishing Co., 1985).

Catalyst. *Catalyst Census of Women Corporate Officers and Top Earners* (New York: Catalyst, 1996).

Catalyst. *On the Line: Women's Career Advancement* (New York: Catalyst, 1992).

Cavender, Cathy. "Networking News: The One Minute Mentor." *Working Woman*, July 1990, p. 13.

Cocola, Nancy Wasserman, and Arlene Modica Matthews. *How to Manage Your Mother: Skills and Strategies to Improve Mother-Daughter Relationships* (New York: Simon & Schuster, 1992).

Crandell, Susan. "The Joys (& Payoffs) of Mentoring." *Executive Female*, March/April 1994.

Bibliography

Daresh, John C., and Marsha A. Playko. *The Professional Development of School Administrators* (New York: Simon & Schuster, 1992).

Davar, Tamina. "Lighting the Path to Success: Mentoring for Asian American Women." *In Careers and the Woman MBA* 2, no. 1. Crimson & Brown Associates. (This article was reprinted from *Inside Asian America*, February/March 1996.)

Dobnrzynski, Judith H. "Somber News for Women on Corporate Ladder." *New York Times*, November 6, 1996.

Dreher, George F., and Ronald A. Ash. "A Comparative Study of Mentoring Among Men and Women in Managerial, Professional, and Technical Positions." *Journal of Applied Psychology* 75, no. 5 (1990): 539–546.

Driscoll, Dawn-Marie, and Carol R. Goldberg. *Members of the Club: The Coming of Age of Executive Women* (New York: Free Press, 1993).

Duff, Carolyn S., and Barbara Cohen. *When Women Work Together: Using Our Strengths to Overcome Our Challenges* (Berkeley, Calif.: Conari Press).

Dunbar, Donette. "Desperately Seeking Mentors." *Black Enterprise*, March 1990, p. 53.

Eichenbaum, Louise, and Susie Orbach. *Between Women* (New York: Viking Penguin, 1988).

Ely, Robin. "The Effects of Organizational Demographics and Social Identity on Relationships Among Professional Women." *Administrative Science Quarterly* 39 (1994): 203–238.

———. "The Power in Democracy: Women's Social Constructions of Gender Identity at Work." *Academy of Management Journal* 38, no. 3 (1995): 589–634.

Federal Glass Ceiling Commission. *A Solid Investment: Making Full Use of the Nation's Human Capital:* Recommendations. Washington, D.C., November 1995.

———. *Good for Business: Making Full Use of the Nation's Human Capital:* A Fact-Finding Report. Washington, D.C., March 1995.

Firman, Dorothy, and Julie Firman. *Daughters & Mothers: Healing the Relationship* (New York: Crossroad, 1994).

Gallese, Liz Roman. "Do Women Make Poor Mentors?" *Across the Board*, July/August 1993, pp. 23–26.

Geiger, Adrianne H. "Measures for Mentors." *Training & Development*, February 1992.

Gibbons, Ann. "Key Issue: Mentoring." *Science* 255 (March 13, 1992): 1368, 1369.

"Giving Women the Business: On Winning, Losing, and Leaving the Corporate Game." Forum. *Harper's Magazine*, December 1997.

Godfrey, Joline. *Our Wildest Dreams: Women Entrepreneurs Making Money, Having Fun, Doing Good* (New York: HarperCollins, 1992).

Granfield, Mary. "Mentoring for Money." *Working Woman*, March 1993, p. 12.

Gray, Janet Dreyfus. "Finding, Keeping and Making the Most of Many Mentors." *Women's News*, October 1995.

Hadley, Joyce, and Betsy Sheldon. *The Smart Woman's Guide to Networking* (Franklin Lakes, N.J.: Career Press, 1995).

Helgesen, Sally. *The Web of Inclusion: Building an Organization for Everyone* (New York: Doubleday, 1995).

Hennig, M., and A. Jardim. *The Managerial Woman* (Garden City, N.Y.: Anchor, 1977).

Hill, Linda A. *Becoming a Manager: Mastery of a New Identity.* (New York: Penguin Books, 1993).

Hill, Linda, and Nancy Kamprath. "Beyond the Myth of the Perfect Mentor: Building a Network of Developmental Relationships." Note prepared as the basis for class discussion (Boston: Harvard Business, 1991).

Hochschild, Arlie Russell. *The Time Bind: When Work Becomes Home and Home Becomes Work* (New York: Henry Holt and Company, 1997).

Howard, Rosemary E., and Joan S. Munch. "Mentoring: A Federal Women's Program Initiative." *The Bureaucrat, The Journal for Public Managers*, Fall 1991, pp. 13–14.

Jamieson, Kathleen Hall. *Beyond the Double Bind: Women and Leadership* (New York: Oxford University Press, 1995).

Johnson, Joan C. "With a Little Help From Her Friends." *Nation's Business*, January 1989.

Kanter, Rosabeth Moss. *Men and Women of the Corporation* (New York: Basic Books, 1977).

Klenke, Karin. *Women and Leadership: A Contextual Perspective* (New York: Springer Publishing, 1996).

Kram, Kathy E. *Mentoring at Work: Developmental Relationships in Organizational Life* (Lanham, Md.: University Press of America, Inc., 1988).

LaTeef, Nelda. *Working Women for the 21st Century* (Charlotte, Vt.: Williamson Publishing, 1992).

Logsdon, Janis. "Need Help? Ask Your Mentor." *Journal of Library Administration* 17, no. 3 (1992): 87–99.

Luebkemann, Heinz, and Jacqueline Clemens. "Mentors for Women Entering Administration: A Program That Works." *NASSP Bulletin* 78, no. 559 (1994): 42 (4).

McCall, Morgan W., Jr., Michael M. Lombardo, and Ann M. Morrison. *Lessons of Experience: How Successful Executives Develop on the Job* (New York: Free Press, 1988).

"Mentors and Proteges." *Working Woman*, October 1989, p. 134.

"Mentors Big Help to Women Executives." *USA Today*, August 1991, p. 7.

Morris, Betsy. "Executive Women Confront Midlife Crisis." *Fortune,* September 18, 1995.

Morris, Michele. "Is It Time to Leave Your Mentor?" *Executive Female,* March/April 1992, pp. 40, 42, 43.

Morrison, Ann M., Randall P. White, Ellen Van Velsor, and the Center for Creative Leadership. *Breaking the Glass Ceiling: Can Women Reach the Top of America's Largest Corporations?* updated edition (Reading, Mass.: Addison-Wesley, 1992).

Mosley, Norman R., and others. "Gender Differences in Same-Sex Friendships and Romantic Relationships." Paper presented at the Annual Meeting of the Eastern Psychological Association, Arlington, Va., April 9–12, 1987.

Murray, Margo, with Marna A. Owen. *Beyond the Myths and Magic of Mentoring: How to Facilitate an Effective Mentoring Program* (San Francisco: Jossey-Bass, 1991).

"The New Power of Women's Networks." *Executive Female,* May/June 1995.

Nichols, Nancy A., ed. *Reach for the Top: Women and the Changing Facts of Work Life* (Boston: Harvard Business, 1994).

Office of Educational Research and Improvement, U.S. Department of Education. "Executive Mentoring: Myths, Issues, Strategies." Women's Educational Equality Act (WEEA) Publishing Center, Educational Development Center, Inc., Newton, Mass.

Olson, Gary, and Evelyn Ashton-Jones. "Doing Gender: (En)Gendering Academic Mentoring." *Boston University Journal of Education* 174, no. 3 (1992): 114–127.

Parker, Victoria A., and Kathy E. Kram. "Women Mentoring Women: Creating Conditions for Connection." *Business Horizons,* March/April 1993, pp. 42–51.

Peters, Sharon L. "Corporate Coaching on Call." *USA Today,* May 10, 1996.

Pipher, Mary. *Reviving Ophelia: Saving the Selves of Adolescent Girls* (New York: Ballantine Books, 1994).

Reardon, Kathleen Kelley. *They Don't Get It, Do They? Communication in the Workplace—Closing the Gap Between Women and Men* (Boston: Little, Brown, 1995).

Rosener, Judy B. *America's Competitive Secret: Utilizing Women as a Management Strategy* (New York: Oxford University Press, 1995).

Saltzman, Amy. "Woman Versus Woman: Why Aren't More Female Executives Mentoring Their Junior Counterparts?" *U.S. News and World Report,* March 25, 1996, pp. 50–53.

Sandler, Bernice R. "Women as Mentors: Myths and Commandments." *The Chronicle of Higher Education,* March 10, 1993, p. B3.

Scandura, Terri A. *Mentoring: The Key to Career Success.* American Woman's Society of Certified Public Accountants, 1992.

"Send in the A Team: African American Women Network Their Way to the Top." *Executive Female*, May/June 1995.

Tanton, Morgan, ed., *Women in Management: A Developing Presence* (New York: Routledge, 1994).

Thompson, Ann McKay, and Marcia Donnan Wood. *Management Strategies for Women* (New York: Simon and Schuster, 1980).

Tieger, Paul D., and Barbara Barron-Tieger. *The Art of Speed Reading People* (Boston: Little, Brown, 1998).

Tovor, Dora A. "Rating Corporations for Diversity and Inclusion: A Look at Hispanics in Corporate America." *In Careers and the Woman MBA*. Crimson & Brown Associates.

Van Velsor, Ellen, and Martha W. Hughes. *Gender Differences in the Devleopment of Managers: How Women Managers Learn From Experience* (Greensboro, N.C.: Center for Creative Leadership, 1990).

Walsh, Elsa. *Divided Lives: The Public and Private Struggles of 3 Accomplished Women* (New York: Simon & Schuster, 1995).

Walsh, Mary Roth, ed. *Women, Men, and Gender: Ongoing Debates* (New Haven, Conn.: Yale University Press, 1997).

Weaver, Vanessa J., and Jan C. Hill. *Smart Women, Smart Moves.* (New York: AMACOM, 1994).

Wickman, Floyd, and Terri Sjodin. *Mentoring: The Most Obvious yet Overlooked Key to Achieving More in Life Than You Dreamed Possible* (Burr Ridge, Ill.: Irwin Professional Publishing, 1997).

Zey, Michael G. "A Mentor for All Reasons." *Personnel Journal* 67, no. 1 (January 1988): pp. 46–51.

———. "Mentoring Programs: Making the Right Moves." *Personnel Journal* 64, no. 2 (1985): 53–57.

———. *The Mentor Connection: Strategic Alliances in Corporate Life.* (New Brunswick, N.J.: Transaction Publishers, 1991).

Index

accomplishment, differences in
    level of, 20–21
action groups, 149–151
admiration for potential mentors,
    87–89
advancement, 8
advantage(s) of woman-to-woman
    mentoring, 1–11
  advancement assistance as, 8
  authenticity as, 5–6
  and availability of mentors,
    9–11
  empathy as, 4
  example of, 1–3
  gender-related advice as, 6–8
affiliation groups, 150
affinity groups, 151–154
Amadoir, Exavier, on sharing
    feelings, 5
American Women's Society of
    CPAs (AWSCPA), 145
Annapurna (Arlene Blum), 48
Applegate, Jane, 119
approaching a mentor, 94
asking women to become mentors,
    96–98
assigned mentoring, 78
A Team, 150
Athena, 33–34

AT&T, 36
attitude, 26–29
authenticity, 5–6
Auyer, Andrea, 50–51
availability of women mentors,
    9–11
AWSCPA (American Women's
    Society of CPAs), 145

BCA Resources, 126
Bechtel Women's Initiative
    (BWI), 142–143
behavior, expectations about, 7
Benton, Debra, on friendship and
    mentoring, 108
biases, personal, 26–29
Blum, Arlene, on friendship and
    mentoring, 48–49
boss, interactions with, 74–75
Briles, Judith, on women-to-
    women work relationships,
    24
*The Briles Report on Women in
    Health Care*, 24
Brown, Betty, 126–127
Burges, Amy, on mentoring
    groups, 130, 132
Burton, Juanita Cox
  on critical feedback, 71
  on formal mentoring, 56–58

businesses, women-owned, 10
BWI, *see* Bechtel Women's Initiative.

Canteen, Jeanne, 54–55
career
    advancement in, 18, 81–82
    as function of mentoring,
        32–33
    respect for choice in, 113–116
career success, 8
Catalyst, 6–7, 9, 58, 129, 140–
    141, 147
Chestnutt, Jane, on individual
    performance, 115–116
Children of the West, 151
choosing a mentor, 83–98
    admiration as basis for, 87–89
    and "connections" of mentor,
        89–90
    example of, 88–89
    factors in, 85–87
    and initiation of relationship,
        83–84, 96–98
    and values, 90–96
Clinton, Hillary Rodham, 116
coaches, 132–136
Colley, Sandra, 58
comfort zones, 24
Committee of 200, 144–145
competence, maintaining image
    of, 14–15
competition/competitiveness, 25–
    26, 116–119, 125, 134
Condit, Madeleine, 53
"connections," mentor's, 89–90
connection with mentor, 94–96
constructive feedback, 79–80

consultant mentors, 132–136
contracts, mentoring, 78–79
corporate officers, 9
corporate women's groups,
    140–144
coworkers, relationships with,
    75–76
critiques, 70–71
cross-organizational formal mentoring, 58–59
culture, male/female, 7, 24

Davar, Tamina, 147
"dead even" rule, 19–21, 70
"Decade of the Executive
    Woman" survey, 10, 22
demanding
    being too, 18–19
    fear of appearing, 13–15
demands, workplace, 24
Destructive Woman, stereotype
    of, 23–26
Dickinson, Jean, 151
Dietz, Jody, 141
Dijkstra, Sandra, on mentoring,
    18
directors, 9
doctors, 9
Dominguez, Cari, on mentors, 52
Dun & Bradstreet Information
    Services, 10
Dundon, Susan, on mentors, 49
Duvall, Janet, on coaching, 135

earners, top, 9
Eichenbaum, Louise, on women-
    to-women relationships, 112
Electra Mentoring Connection,
    137

Ely, Robin
  on "Queen Bees," 21
  on women in senior positions,
    25
e-mentoring, 136–137
emotions, 5
empathy, 4
ending mentoring relationships,
    82, 102–103
ethnic groups/networks, 146–149
evaluation of mentors, 98–102
executive vice presidents, 9
expectations
  about behavior, 7
  about women's work relation-
    ships, 23–26
  of mentor, 76–82
  performance, 7

Fairstein, Linda, 151–152
fears of women-to-women mentor-
    ing, 13
  example of, 1–3, 13–14
  and personal bias, 26–29
  see also myth(s) about women-
    to-women mentoring
feedback
  for mentors, 72, 80–81
  for protégés, 70–71, 79–80
feelings, expressing, 5–6
FemLogic, 43
Fire With Fire (Naomi Wolf),
    150–151
Firman, Dorothy, 112
Firman, Julie, 112
Fogelstrom, Pat, 53–54
formal mentoring, 77–79, 83–84
  with assigned mentors, 55–58

cross-organizational opportuni-
    ties for, 58–59
formal mentors, 68–69
Fortune 500 companies, 9, 133
Fortune 2000 companies, 9
fostering, 36
friends, as mentors, 47–50, 77,
    107–111
Furst, Cindy, on formal mentor-
    ing, 56

Gabor, Andrea, 150
Gallup, 10
gays, 141
gender culture, 24
gender-related perceptions/ex-
    pectations, 608
Gift, Rosemary, on mentoring
    groups, 129–130
gift exchange, mentoring as, 4,
    31–60, 72, 156
  examples of, 31–32, 45–47
  and "fit," 47
  with formal mentoring, 55–59
  and friendship, 47–50
  and goals of mentoring, 38–40
  with informal mentoring,
    50–55
  and male mentoring tradition,
    32–34
  and mutual learning, 40–44
  and relationship, 37–38
  and unique features of women-
    to-women mentoring, 34–37
Gilfoyle, Elnora, on Mentoring
    Circles, 130–131
Glaser, Connie, on seeking men-
    tors, 11

glass ceiling, 132, 133
Glass Ceiling Commission, 7
goals
    developing, 77–79
    of mentoring, 38–40
Goodman, Ellen, on friendship
    and mentoring, 49–50
Gordon, Ellen, 144
Gray, Janet Dreyfus, on multiple
    mentors, 63
Grogan, Barbara, on friendship
    and mentoring, 48
groups, 128–131
    action, 149–151
    affiliation, 150
    affinity, 151–154
    corporate, 140–144
    ethnic/cultural, 146–149
    resource, 150

Hach, Kathryn, 145
Heffner, Christy, 144
Heim, Pat, on "dead even" rule,
    20
Helgesen, Sally, on unnamed
    mentoring relationships, 51
Hewlett-Packard, 56, 143
hierarchy, 69–70
Hill, Linda
    on being a successful protégé,
        65–66
    on peer relationships,
        124–125
Hobbs, Eleanor, on female men-
    toring, 38–39
Homer, 32, 33, 35
horizontal mentoring, 127–128

Ibarra, Hermania, on gender-
    related career advice, 6

influential positions, 8
informal mentoring, 77–78
    with named mentoring connec-
        tion, 53–55
    with unnamed coach/advocate,
        50–53
informal mentors, 64–65, 68–69
initiation of mentoring relation-
    ship, 83–84, 96–98
initiative, taking, 156
Internet, 136–137
intimacy, 108–109

Jansen, Sue Curry, on mentoring,
    35
Jeruchim, Joan, 8
job satisfaction, 8
John Hancock Mutual Life Insur-
    ance Company, 58
Jordan, Joyce, on coaches, 134

Kanter, Rosabeth Moss, 144
Kodak Women's Forum, 141
Korn/Ferry International, 10
Kram, Kathy
    on career/lifestyle choices, 115
    on mentoring, 32–33
    on peer mentoring, 123–124
Kusumoto, Ann, 147

lawyers, 9, 25
learning connection, 68–69
    and friendship, 48
    initiation of, 16–17
    and mutual learning, 40–44
    refusal of, 17, 19
Lenke, Larin, on mentoring risks,
    66
lesbians, 141

Lester, Joan
　on action groups, 150
　on corporate mentoring groups,
　　141
Levine, Tara, on mentoring net-
　works, 144
lifestyle/career choices, respect
　for, 113–116
liking others, 94
Linder, Kitty, 54–55

male mentors, xiv–xv
　and advancement, 8
　and expression of feelings, 5
managers, 9
McMillan, Micki, on coaching,
　135
men, peer relationships between,
　20, 38
Mentor (Homerian character), 32,
　33, 35
Mentoring and Work (Kathy
　Kram), 32–33, 123–124
Mentoring Circles, 130–131
mentoring groups, *see* groups.
"MentorNet," 137
mentors, *see under specific head-
　ings, e.g.,* choosing a
　mentor.
Menttium 100, 137
Morgan, Robin, on sisterhood, 35
Morris, Betsy, on midlife crisis,
　152–153
Morton, Karen, 58
"mother/daughter" issues,
　111–113
multiple mentors, 63–65
mutuality, 21, 72

mutual learning, 40–44
myth(s) about women-to-women
　mentoring, 16–29
　"dead even" rule as, 19–21
　Destructive Woman as, 23–26
　likelihood of rejection as,
　　16–17
　and personal bias, 26–29
　Queen Bee as, 21–22
　right to be mentored as, 18–19

National Association of Women
　Business Owners, 118–119
National Foundation for Women
　Business Owners, 10
National Organization of Business
　Women, 144
needy, fear of appearing, 13–15
networks, women's, 140
　exclusion from, 19
　as mentors, 65
NYNEX, 81–82, 129

obstacles, 7
Odyssey (Homer), 32, 33, 35
officers, corporate, 9
on-line, finding mentors,
　136–137
Orbach, Susie, on women-to-
　women relationships, 112
Otte, Jean, 58–59

Parker, Victoria A., on career/
　lifestyle choices, 115
partnership, 72
Pashkow, Peg, on mentoring the
　whole person, 39–40
Pebley, Mary, 9

Pedelty, Lori
on coaching, 134–135
on women's career needs,
135–136
peer mentors, 123–127
perceptions, gender-related, 6–7
performance
as advancement criterion, 8
expectations of, 7
personal biases, 26–29
"Perspective: A Case for Mentoring Women," 6
Peters, Sharon L., on corporate
coaching, 134
Phillips, Sue, on informal mentoring, 52–53
politics, situational, 16
Popcorn, Faith, on FemLogic, 43
positions held by women, 9
potential, as advancement criterion, 8
power, women in positions of,
25–26
power groups, 149–151
Price, Courtney, on avoiding competition, 119
primary mentors, 64
promotions, 18, 81–82
protection of mentoring relationship, 105–120
and competition, 116–119
example of, 105–106
and friendship issue, 107–111
and "mother/daughter" issues,
111–113
and respect for career/lifestyle
choices, 113–116
protégé(s), 61–82
accomplished women as teachers of, 68–69

becoming a, 65–68
and boss, 74–75
constructive feedback for,
79–80
and coworkers, 75–76
and critique, 70–71
example of, 61–63
and expectations of mentor,
76–82
goals of, 77–79
and hierarchy, 69–70
multiple mentors for, 63–65
and other obligations of mentor, 73–74
promotions for, 81–82
response to opportunities by,
81
role of, 71–73
support of mentor by, 73,
80–81
thanking of mentor by, 82
psychosocial functions of mentoring, 33

Queen Bee, myth of, 21–22

reciprocity, 71–73
rejection
fear of, 16–18
by mentors, 18–19
relationship, as foundation of
women-to-women mentoring, 37–38
resentment from others, 75
resource groups, 150
respect, 15
right to be mentored, 18–19
risk of mentoring, 66

Rodick, Anita, 132
Rosener, Judy, on informal mentoring, 69

sabotage, workplace, 24
satisfaction, job, 8
Schaef, Anne Wilson, on peer relationships between women, 20, 38, 108
secondary mentors, 64
selecting a mentor, *see* choosing a mentor.
self-esteem, 5, 8
senior vice presidents, 9
Shapiro, Pat, 8
sharing mentoring experiences, 139–156
  in action/power groups, 149–151
  in affinity groups, 151–154
  in corporate forums, 140–144
  in ethnic groups/networks, 146–149
  and future of women in workplace, 154–156
  in networks, 140
  outside of the corporation, 144–146
Shields, Vickie Rutledge, 109–110
short-term mentors, 122–123
Sisterhood is Powerful (Robin Morgan), 35
Sjodin, Terri L., on primary/secondary mentors, 63–64
Skogg, Susan
  on community, 156
  on learning from women, xiv

Small Business Administration, 59
Solver, A. David, on women hiring women, 10
statistics on woman-to-woman mentoring, 9–10, 22, 140–141
Strickland, Stephanie, on fostering, 36
style, developing an effective, 7–8
success
  career, 8
  factors in, 6–7
superior mentors, 64
support for mentor, showing, 73, 80–81
Swim With the Dolphins (Connie Glaser), 11

Taking Charge (Joan Lester), 150
Tannen, Deborah, on rapport between women, 20
teaching, 92
thanking mentors, 82
traditional mentoring, 33
Turner, Caroline, 132

unnamed mentoring relationships, 50–53
U.S. Bureau of Statistics, 9
U.S. News and World Report, 9
US West, 57–58

Valentine, Nancy, 146
values, shared, 90–96
vice presidents, 9
Vilar, Maria, 39

Vincent, Marjorie, on peer mentors, 123, 126

Walkland, Holly, 141
The Wall Street Journal, 7, 10
Ward-Collins, Diana, 53–54
weak, fear of appearing, 13–15
Wedge, Karen
  on mentoring, 35
  on values, 94
weekend mentoring, 131–132
Wellington, Sheila, on success
  factors, 6–7
wholeness, 4
Why Women Work Together
  (Carolyn Duff), 23, 24
Wickman, Floyd, on primary/secondary mentors, 63–64
WIN (Women's Information Network), 143
Wolf, Naomi, on action groups,
  150–151
A Woman's Reality (Anne Wilson
  Schaef), 38, 108

woman-to-woman, xv–xvi
woman-to-woman mentoring
  statistics on, 9–10
Woman to Woman Mentoring Program, 137
Women, Mentors and Success
  (Joan Jeruchim and Pat
  Shapiro), 8
women of color, 93, 137,
  146–149
women-owned businesses, 10
Women's Information Network
  (WIN), 143
"womentoring," 36–37
Women Unlimited, 58–59
workforce, in women-owned companies, 10
Working Woman magazine, 10
WOW'M: The Mentoring Company, 130, 132

Yancy, Jean, on mentoring,
  35–36